THE COMPLETE COIN COLLECTING GUIDE FOR BEGINNERS

Easy-to-Follow Practical Advice to Build your Coin Collection & Uncover your Coin's Actual Value

Franklin Morgan

TABLE OF CONTENTS

BOOK 1: COIN COLLECTING 101

Introduction

This book is part of a series of how-to guides related to coin collecting. In this guide, the first to be more precise, you will be provided with all the basic knowledge relating to coins, their identikit and coinage. We will also introduce you to the world of numismatics, and its origins.

Coin collecting today is a very widespread practice that involves more and more people in the world. And it is for this reason that we have decided to bring more and more people to the knowledge of this art, both ancient and modern.

For this form of hobby, art or business, we refer; in fact, to that form of collecting and commerce that concerns coins or other forms of legally issued currencies. It is therefore a safe, legal activity that will also give you satisfaction. So, this first book was therefore written in order to bring you to the knowledge of the world of coins, how they are formed, and from which bases to start to be able to create a profitable coin collection and make it a business.

Thanks to this guide, you will also be offered the possibility of being able to understand which the best coins are to collect and therefore, consequently, also which ones to discard.

Specifically, this first guide will be divided into 4 parts:

- In the first part of the book, we want to give you some good advice before starting: we will show you the anatomy of a coin and from what parts is it formed. All are accompanied by a terms glossary in which you will find a complete list with coin-collecting terms in alphabetic order.

- In the second part of the book, we will talk about real coinage: from the origin of coins to how/why people started to collect coins. There will also be a dedicated section to the modern minting process, which are the precise steps to create a coins

- Part three will be totally dedicated to "Numismatics": we will explain what is and where the term comes from, with some Numismatics facts too.

- In the final part, we will start to talk about coin collection basics : we will show you some reasons why to start collecting coins today. This together with the different collectible types of coins (bullion, commemorative, circulating, uncirculated, medals, etc.). This book will end with some pros and Cons of Coin Collecting as a business.

We are quite sure that, at the end of reading this text, you will have all the tools to understand if a coin collection could be right for you and to start this possible future business in the best way or to evaluate it as a very useful hobby also for involving members of your family or friends.

CHAPTER 1: BEFORE STARTING TO COLLECT COINS

In this first "cognitive" chapter we will show you everything you need to know about coins, their structure (how they are made, in other words) and the meaning of each single collecting term.

Anatomy of a Coin

In this first paragraph, we will explain the various parts of the coins. In reality, this paragraph will be divided into two parts: in the first, we will explain the meaning of money, while in the second we will talk about the various parts of which it is made up.

Meaning of the word Coin

Let's start with the term money itself: By money, in a general sense we mean everything that is used as a means of payment and intermediary of commercial exchanges. But, as we will see, the coin is also a tool for creating a collection also for the purpose of making money.

In general, however, we can say that money, both from its origins, also currently performs the functions of:

✓ The measure of value (money as a unit of account).

✓ Means of exchange in the sale of goods and services and in commercial transactions in general (currency as a payment instrument).

✓ Fund of value (currency as a store of value).

Therefore, the main function of money is that of a payment instrument, given that the other functions are either a consequence of it or a favorable condition for its performance.

The distinction between a unit of account and means of payment was more evident in ancient economies when there were "virtual" currencies, today we would say scriptural, (such as the talent, the medieval lira, and so on…) which did not physically exist and were not minted, but they were used only to count and stipulate contracts (unit of account); real coins (means of payment) were used to settle the bond.

In numismatics, and we will see it specifically in the third chapter of this guide, money is understood in the sense of a specific material object, generally metal disks representing money, which can be current or out-of-circulation currency.

But, without going into numismatics too specifically, which we will do later, it is important for a moment to make a small but really important distinction between the concept of money and that of currency.

In essence, money represents the currency accepted by the market, i.e., by anyone, in a given historical period. Telephone tokens, mini cheques from the 1970s, candies given as change at the bar, and the hours of Ithaca (New York) are an example of money. In antiquity, before the birth of money in the strict sense, money consisted of objects of various kinds and more: cocoa beans, shells, iron bars, skewers, salt (hence wages), livestock (hence pecuniary), cakes of tea and so on. This primitive currency, anthropologists point out, was actually a "social currency", i.e. it was not used to buy and sell goods, but to create, maintain and reorganize relationships between people, for example, to contract marriages or to obtain pardon in case of a crime.

Money (strictly speaking) is the currency issued by the State, always in each and precise historical period. It belongs to the money category until it is accepted by the market: coins that are out of circulation and devalued coins are no longer money because nobody accepts them.

To put it in more technical terms, a coin is nothing more than a metal disk minted, in order to facilitate exchanges, by state authorities which guarantee its alloy, fineness, weight and established value: Among the typical expressions relating to coins and some more singular uses we have:

✓ A nice hoard of gold coins.

✓ Collection of coins.

✓ Throw the coin to decide fate or to take any decision, making "heads or tails".

To summarize what we have said so far, the concept of coins has always been seen with a collective value, but with a broader meaning, the set of everything which, in a given country and in a given period, is accepted as a means of payment, and therefore used as an intermediary of exchange, a measure of values and store of value; from a historical point of view, money is presented as a particular commodity which, in cultures of historical periods following the barter phase, is chosen to represent the values of all the other commodities according to quantitative ratios defined from time to time, and which originally can consist of various goods (livestock, hides, shells, salt, etc.), then almost universally replaced by gold and other precious metals (due to their characteristics of scarcity, transferability, inalterability, homogeneity, divisibility) in powder form, ingots and finally minted in different shapes. Having done this identikit of the coin, let's analyze its anatomy.

Parts of the coin

Well, let's now see which parts are at the base of the anatomy of a coin. First of all, we tell you that as a fundamental part of the coin production process, the choice of materials comes first. The materials chosen to make the metal blanks must have precise characteristics. Good ductility guarantees the reproducibility of the design on the blank, avoiding excessive wear of the coining dies. A high resistance to wear and corrosion allows one to obtain durable coins, reducing the loss of luster over time.

Coins must also be safe from the point of view of health: the use of nickel is limited, which triggers allergic reactions in sensitive subjects, and there is a tendency to use copper and its alloys for their antibacterial properties. Fighting counterfeiting is also of vital importance: therefore, coins with particular magnetic and surface properties are produced, which are difficult to reproduce outside the official Mints. Finally, it is essential that the cost of production does not exceed the face value of the coin. Other than that, what are the most used materials? A statistical study has shown that, to date, the most used materials to produce currency in the world are, in descending order: steel (30%), stainless steel (27%), nickel (18%), aluminum (17 %), brass (13%), cupronickel (12%), copper (8%), aluminum bronze (3%), Nordic gold (2%). Multiple materials can be used in combination to produce the same coin, such as bi-metal or plated ones - which is why the reported percentages add up to over 100%.

Materials with lower corrosion resistance and less expensive (such as steel) are used as the core, to be plated with more expensive materials with good surface properties (copper, nickel...). While stainless steel, aluminum and copper alloys are mainly used as the sole constituent of the blank.

Having described the materials from which it is made, let's now see the various parts that make up a coin. The coin is first of all a multi-screen system, with two faces: the obverse and the reverse, and then the one with the edge which I consider the third face.

In these screens (faces) there are different areas in which we can find writing, numbers and symbols.

✓ Rim: is the outer edge, the border, and often the relief.

✓ Round: is the part near the edge where a legend usually appears.

✓ Exergues: the underside of the coin where the mintmark or date appears.

✓ Edge: is the external part that forms the thickness; it can be smooth, lined or worked in various ways

✓ Field: is the free space between Type and Legend where symbols, abbreviations or writings can appear

✓ Type: is the main figure, usually the image of a ruler or a personality

✓ Legend: is the main entry

✓ Imprint: is given by the Type and the Legend. The imprint is the main message that celebrates a subject or an event. To better explain the concept of a fingerprint, let's take the Kennedy half a dollar for example. The inscription LIBERTY (legend) which has always been a word-symbol of the USA and the image of President JF Kennedy (type), is the imprint of this coin which celebrates the president assassinated the previous year.

There is a variety of information that we can read on coins and these, together with the imprint, the metal used, the size and weight, form the monetary message as a whole. A high-sounding sentence the latter but profoundly true and serious. Coins tell us much more than just their face value and, in some ways, even more than the imprint itself. So next time you look at a coin, whether it's contemporary, out of circulation, or ancient, remember you're looking at a communication system; so, look for the message and the varied information it conveys.

Terms Glossary: Alphabetic List of Coin Collecting Terms

We conclude this first part of the guide with a glossary entirely dedicated to coin collecting.

✓ Adequate:

The average price of a commodity; an average of prices for various years or markets; the average value of different coins.

✓ Bimetallic Coin

The coin is produced through the use of two different metals.

✓ Brilliant Uncirculated

A coin that never entered circulation and was carefully preserved immediately after its minting. It may present at most very slight marks due to contact with other coins during the production process. It is the highest degree of conservation because it comes from limited editions intended for collecting. 10/10 of metal is present in the reliefs.

✓ Circulation

A number of coins minted in a year for every single coin.

✓ Common Side

The side of the coin common to all countries corresponds to the Value Side.

✓ Coinage defect

A coinage defect is a general imperfection of various kinds caused by a mistake using a damaged or simply dirty coinage.

✓ Coin measure

Which can serve as a term of comparison in the measurement of the value of other currencies as it has stable content; the expression entered the economic language to indicate the set of bank accounts and deposits that cannot be used on demand, cash vouchers and ordinary vouchers of the Treasury in the short term, as they can fulfill some of the monetary functions alongside real money.

✓ Coinage

Process of manufacturing metal coins, which consists in impressing signs or symbols on both sides of the coins, and sometimes also on the edges, so as to make it difficult to counterfeit and shear or erode.

✓ Coining

Producing a coin using a coinage.

✓ Collecting

Collecting is a hobby that consists of collecting objects of a particular category. The set of collected objects is called a collection. In the case of coins, precisely, it is defined as coin collecting.

✓ Countermark

Ticket or token that serves as a marker. Sign affixed by the issuing authority on the obverse or reverse of the coin after its issue, to increase or decrease its value and, if necessary, to put coins already withdrawn back into circulation. To countermark: it means to mark with a countermark, to put a countermark.

✓ Denomination side

The face of the coin with the face value.

✓ Embossment

Part of the coin with design in relief with respect to the field of the coin.

✓ Exergue

The lower part of the coin is where the value and date are usually engraved.

✓ Exonumia

The sector of Numismatics is the study of numismatic objects such as Tokens, Medals or Engravings.

✓ Face value

Value of the coin engraved on it.

✓ Fake

Fake money is passed off as real.

✓ Flan

Smooth metal coin ready to strike.

✓ Foot

In the minting of coins, the foot (of the coin) is called the number of pieces that can be minted with the unit of weight (usually, in countries with a metric system, one kilogram) of the relative fine metal.

✓ Gipsoteca

Collection of models and plaster casts of sculptures or architectural parts, especially from classical antiquity (in which case it constitutes a means [...] of study, and is usually housed in universities or academies), or of individual artists (such as the plaster cast gallery of Possagno, which collects casts and plaster models of works by A. Canova); there are also plaster casts with casts of coins and gems.

✓ Hybrid

A coin that has the face of two different coins.

✓ Incuse

Part of the engraved design is recessed with respect to the surface of the coin itself.

✓ Intrinsic coin value

By value or purchasing power of money, we mean the number of goods and services that can be purchased with it. The intrinsic value of a coin is the value of the instrument (for example, the metal coin or the bank note) used as money. It depends on the value of the asset that makes up the currency.

✓ Lapping

The technique of preparation of the blanks for the minting of Proof coins.

✓ Mint

A mint is a workshop that produces coins, banknotes, stamps and seals of a state [. The word comes from the Arabic سكة, pronounced Sikka, literally "mint".

Overall, the history of mints is very closely linked with the history of coins, although the former is more connected to short-term politics than the latter.

✓ Minting

An instrument for beating the flans used for the production of coins.

✓ Molten Coin

The coin is produced by casting metal on the negative mold.

✓ Monetary

Concerning coins, relating to coins: monetary circulation between several states; monetary theories; a forgery of coins.

✓ Monetary policy

It is distinguished into external currency, the one introduced into the economic system by the monetary authorities; and the internal one, the one that enters circulation through the operation of the banking system; single currency, adopted in several countries following international agreements.

✓ Monetary system

The set of currencies circulating at a given moment in a state, i.e. the monetary unit and its multiples and submultiples; until 1999, the European Monetary System, often indicated with the acronym SME agreement between the countries of the EEC (now EU, European Union), to determine the guide changes and the fluctuation band of the various currencies, then replaced by the European Monetary Union Aureus or silver monetary system, if the monetary unit is a currency respectively gold or silver and if the circulation consists only of standard coins and coin denominations or also of convertible banknotes; monetary system bimetallic, bimetallism system: with a gold exchange if the circulation is made up only of bills convertible into gold bullion, or of foreign currencies in turn convertible into gold and of coin denominations.

✓ National Side

The side of the Euro coin is personalized by the individual issuing country.

✓ Numismatic

A historical, artistic, geographical and economic study of Coins / Coin Collecting

✓ Obverse

The face of the coin with the most prominent design is usually where the issuing authority is indicated.

✓ Outline:

The edge is part of the coin between the Obverse and the Reverse. The thickness of the coin.

✓ Patina:

A film forms over the coin due to the oxidation of the metal.

✓ Proof

Flan struck before minting to verify the design of the new coin.

✓ Re-minting

Coin struck through original minting but on a date after the year of issue.

✓ Reproduction

Faithful imitation of a coin with less precious metal. Usually signed.

✓ Reverse

Also called the Reverse or Value Side, it is the face of the coin opposite to the Obverse.

✓ Rising

Manner and act of rising. Referred to coins, in economic language, the increase in their price without an equal increase in the fine content.

✓ Rotation axes

The ratio between the axes of the two sides of the coin. It is measured in degrees.

✓ Shearing

The ancient fraudulent practice was to remove precious metals from coins by filing them on the sides.

✓ Sides:

The sides are the two opposite sides of the coin.

✓ Spin

Of money, circulating it has been a long time since gold coins have circulated; it seems that there are fake tickets; writings, and news. Spread among the public.

✓ Test Design

Experimental designs for new coins were minted to test their effect and yield.

CHAPTER 2: THE COINAGE

In this second chapter, we will deal with real coinage. We will analyze its origin and current meaning today.

Origin of Coins

In this paragraph, we will take care of indicating you a brief history of the first's coins in the world and how it has continued over time.

In our daily lives, money is essentially a payment instrument, a medium of exchange with which we pay and are paid.

The coin itself is a relatively recent invention, occurring around the middle of the 6th century BC.

Before the appearance of the currency, the management of exchanges was carried out through reciprocity or barter, subsequently with natural currency or commodity-money and finally with metal-tools. It is believed that it was the need to manage increasingly intense trade that determined the final diffusion of money, but not everyone shares this "straight-line" view of the birth of money following the needs of the exchange/market economy.

But, in reality, the coin had and still has other functions, but none of these can be traced from the etymology of its name which is particularly fascinating, and which is due to the famous story of the Capitoline geese.

In 390 BC. Rome was under siege by the Gauls of Brennus; on the citadel of the Campidoglio, there was the temple of Juno where the geese sacred to the goddess were raised.

One night, when the Gauls arrived, the geese started squawking and woke up the ex-consul Marco Manlio who sounded the alarm. The attack was then thwarted thanks to the sacred geese. Manlius added the cognomen Capitolinus to his name.

From that moment on, the goddess Juno acquired the appellative of Moneta, from the Latin verb money which stands for warn, admonish, as it was believed that she had awakened her geese to warn of the arrival of the Gauls.

Subsequently, around 269 BC, the mint was built near the temple of Juno Moneta on Capitoline Hill and placed right under the protection of the goddess Moneta. At that point, it was the popular language that transmitted the appellation of the Goddess first to the mint and then to what was produced there.

The nomisma of the Greeks and the nummus of the Latins, therefore, became money.

But returning to the transition from barter to coins, with the birth of agricultural economies, the greater sedentary lifestyle and organization of work made the need for a more articulated trading system than barter increasingly evident. As the frequency of exchanges increases, it, therefore, becomes necessary that an instrument accepted in payment by all economic operators comes into play, consisting in fact of goods with their own intrinsic value: This commodity currency (or commodity-sample or natural currency) could be extremely varied but had to fulfill some specific characteristics in order to act as a means of exchange (and therefore "currency" in the broadest sense):

✓ Non-perishability is a characteristic that allows its value to be preserved over time (otherwise part of the acceptance would be lost) and favors its hoarding in anticipation of desired but uncertain future exchanges.

✓ Availability encourages its diffusion in exchanges, which leads to widespread acceptance, which leads to further diffusion, triggering a multiplicative mechanism. Obviously, we mean something widespread but not abundant in a broad sense.

✓ Verifiability is a feature that reduces payment uncertainties and thus increases the acceptance of such assets as a means of payment release.

✓ Divisibility, the commodity-money must be divisible to some extent.

Even some great civilizations or in any case civilizations equipped with writing continued to use goods as money until recent times or when alternative forms of coinage existed. In the Latin world cattle and slaves were of great importance; in Japan, where rice remained the unit of account of the great fiefdoms until their abolition; in 1868, in Iceland, the equivalent of dried fish was established for each commodity until the 19th century (but China also used real ingots, silver taels, until the 1930s).

Money is therefore an abstract and evolved form of payment, i.e., a counterpart to a good or service that replaces bartering and at the same time offers ample flexibility to purchase any other type of good, even fractional, at the price of its respective value, which is determined by the interaction of four factors: cost of production, utility, supply and demand.

The first coin of history

In the economies of the ancient Mediterranean and India, precious metals established themselves as means of payment, especially with their transformation into gold, silver and copper coins.

Tradition has it that the coin was minted for the first time by Croesus, king of Lydia, in the 6th century BC. In the following century, the custom of minting coins spread to the Persian Empire and the Greek cities. Then, through the Greeks, the use of coins was introduced in the Western Mediterranean. Finally, in the time of Alexander the Great, it also spread to India.

Anthropologist David Graeber speaks of the "slave military coinage complex to indicate the historically present link between coinage and violence. The first coins were minted by the ancient States to hire and pay the soldiers of their armies; the effect of wars and conquests are looting and thefts, mainly consisting of gold, silver, and bronze, hoarded in temples and in the houses of landowners, metals that are melted down to obtain coins ("anonymous" and transportable goods); another effect of war is slavery', and one of the main tasks of slaves was precisely to extract precious metals from the mines; finally, tributes in money are imposed on the populations, especially those conquered, which thus returns to the rulers. The money markets are an indirect effect of all these processes.

In some civilizations, only one of the two precious metals has been used because to Gresham's law «In a country with two legal currencies in circulation, the bad drives out the good, when the real relationship between them changes». For example, in China, India, Russia, and Persia only silver coins were used. In the Mediterranean, unified starting from the Roman Empire, gold coinage prevailed. Copper was used in all these territories for coins of lesser value.

How did People Start to Collect Coins?

Now let's see how coin collecting was born. Since ancient times, non-intrinsic peculiarities have been reserved for money in its economic function as a means of exchange. Greek coins, small masterpieces of ancient engraving, enchant us with their refined beauty; Roman coins "carried" throughout the Empire the messages that the emperor wanted to convey from time to time to his subjects; an "offer" was placed in the mouth of the deceased so that they could pay for the passage on the ferry to Charon, imperial coins were found affixed to the niches of the first Christians in the Roman catacombs, a coin was placed in the foundations of new construction to mark the beginning. Collecting coins, therefore, is not just collecting different specimens, but it is reliving all of this, going back in time and space, and keeping a fragment of what has been our history, the History of Man, in a small piece of metal. One of the oldest forms of collecting is undoubtedly numismatics.

If we are to believe the descriptions of the Roman historian Suetonius (70-140 AD), the emperor Augustus was one of the first to collect "royal and foreign coins" more than 2000 years ago. Other cases of collections and collectors in the Roman period are reported; Unlike other works of art, the focus of attention in coin collecting was not always the aesthetic aspect.

The passion for collecting coins dates back to the Roman emperors, as was common in the late ancient period to use a coin as a pendant to be set in a choker. Real numismatic collecting sees its beginning with Humanism, being part of that renewed interest in the ancient world. The initiator of numismatic studies is Francesco Petrarca, who was the first to consider coins as a means of historical study, as we learn from his Letters. However, the first great collector of Roman coins was Cardinal Pietro Barbo, the future Pope Paul II; another great collector was Cosimo de Medici. The most important private collection in the last century was that of the very rich collection of King Vittorio Emanuele III, donated to Italy and now kept in the Medagliere of Palazzo Massimo.

In short, collecting coins has been a passion present since ancient times until today. As we said in the introduction, coin collecting is a very common practice today.

Modern Coining Process: Steps to Create a Coins

We close this chapter on the origins of coin collecting by examining what are the steps for modern coinage. We want you to remember that coin striking (or minting) is the process of transferring a design from a die to a metal blank. It takes its name from the conî, metal punches that bear the negative images created by the engravers chosen to mark the coins. Each coin is obtained with two dies, one for the obverse and one for the reverse.

But before we look at the steps for minting coins, let's briefly see how this process has evolved in modern times until today.

✓ Issuance in a system with coins only

Until the 19th century, metal coins minted using precious metals were in circulation almost exclusively. Money was created by bringing the raw metal to the mint, usually owned or licensed by the state, where the coins were minted. The precious metal came from the mines and from abroad, following positive trade balances, and settled using precious metals.

The quantity of money circulating in the economy could therefore increase or decrease, in the case of trade deficits regulated by the sale of precious metals, not compensated by the new mining extractions. Changes in the number of coins affected prices. Prices rose or fell (deflation) with the quantity of money and with effects that affected wages and employment.

✓ The issuance of money by banks

In the late Middle Ages, the evolution of the economy led to the creation, alongside metal coins, of bank money (not to be confused with bank money understood as the set of payment instruments provided today by banks, in addition to legal money in circulation). The deposit of surplus gold with goldsmiths, some of whom become bankers and lend the precious metal received and not held as reserves, favors the birth of a credit system, in which the bankers' liabilities become money. Each bank ends up issuing its own currency, which is accepted in payment only if the bank is deemed solvent.

✓ The creation of money by the central bank

The multiplicity of currencies and issuers, a source of instability and periodic financial crises, was tackled starting from the seventeenth century by deciding to concentrate the power to issue money in the hands of a single subject, the central bank.

This limits the power to grant credit by the banks, which cannot exceed the limit imposed on them by the obligation to hold part of the funding in the form of reserves (today no longer in gold but in extremely liquid assets), and the central bank is given the power to refinance banks, when necessary. This power serves both to increase the money supply, through the increase in the monetary base by the central bank, and to guarantee the solvency of the banks.

So, having seen the process of modern coinage, how are coins minted? Let's see it together:

There are basically two main coining techniques: hammer and mechanical.

- ✓ Hammer minting was the oldest form of coin production. Hammered coins were made by placing a smooth metal disc, the flan, between two cones. Then the upper die was struck with a hammer to impress the required image on both sides of the coin.

- ✓ Mechanical coinage is the coining carried out with the aid of a machine, generally a press. The first coins of this type were produced on an experimental basis in the mid-16th century in England, while in Italy they saw the light between 1608 and 1620, in the Grand Duchy of Tuscany; the total abandonment of hammer minting occurred only with the Italian unification and the diffusion of the single currency, the Lira.

- ✓ Today the process of creating the conî requires a few steps: the artist creates a large plaster model of the coin; this is then covered with silicone rubber to create a negative mold used to make a positive copy of the coin in metal or resin. With a pantograph, the image is reduced on a positive steel matrix and from this matrix, the working dies are created, to strike the coins.

- ✓ The rubber mold is then used to make a metal copy. All this takes place on a model of about 20 cm in diameter. Then, with a pantograph, it takes several days to reduce the image onto a positive steel matrix in a process that hasn't changed in about a hundred years. The positive matrix is then tempered to make it hard. Then a small number of die stamps (incuses) are made starting from the positive die. These are then used to make the work positive. The working positives are then used to make the working dies. With each pass, the number of pieces increases. The working dies are finally used to strike coins. All dies are incuse, and all positives resemble the coin that will be minted.

- ✓ The final step, of course, is striking the dies used to imprint the image onto the flan to form the final coin.

- ✓ Of course, errors can occur at all stages of this production process and these errors are particularly sought after by collectors. Mistakes present in minting are generally more in demand than errors made at the time of striking. For example, a doubled die, in which a date or other element appears twice somewhat offset, is often highly sought after. Typing errors are usually unique, while all coins struck with an incorrect minting will have the same characteristics. This makes them easier to collect. The most famous doubled coin in America during the last hundred years is the double coin struck in 1955 on the Lincoln cent.

- ✓ There is also a third way to produce medals alone: fusion. It consists in pouring molten metal into a matrix bearing the type of the obverse and the reverse.

Our general discourse on coins, their structure, their creation and their history concludes with passages relating to modern minting. From the next chapter onwards, we will talk about real coin collecting.

CHAPTER 3: NUMISMATICS

When we talk about coin collecting, we cannot fail to mention numismatics. In this third part of the book, we will deal with describing all the essential features and all the facts.

Understanding Numismatics

Now, let's explain what numismatics is and where the term comes from. When we talk about numismatics, we refer to the scientific study of money and its history, in all its various forms, from a historical-geographical, artistic and economic point of view. As far as we are specifically concerned in this guide, it must be said that, often, coin collecting is also referred to as numismatics and for this reason, the two concepts coincide. As regards the origin of the term itself, numismatics derives from the Latin numismatic, in turn from the Greek: νόμισμα – nomisma – i.e., coin.

From the definition we have just given you, the most important object of numismatics is the coin. But this science is also interested in other forms of money, such as banknotes, pre-monetary means of payment and coin-shaped objects such as medals, medallions, tokens and religious tags.

Numismatics can also include the study of many different aspects related to coins, including history, geography, economics, metallurgy, use and production processes.

Other payment methods, such as checks, banknotes, paper money, scripophily and credit cards are also often objects of numismatic interest. Even the first coins or pre-coins used by primitive peoples are part of the study of numismatics.

Furthermore, numismatics can be considered a typical museum science (Bernd Kluge), since significant works are mostly only possible with material sources, i.e., coins. The large public numismatic collections have therefore also been research centers and are still the promoters of large cataloging works and compendiums. Among the most important numismatic collections, there are those in Paris (National Library), London (British Museum), New York (American Numismatic Society), Berlin (Münzkabinett), the numismatic cabinet at the Kunsthistorisches Museum in Vienna. Last but not least, we should mention the former royal collection of Vittorio Emanuele III, the numismatist king who, on his departure into exile, was donated to the Italian state. Today it is exhibited in Rome, in the (Palazzo Massimo alle Terme).

Numismatics does not work intensively only in museums: its very genesis is linked to the world of collecting which still today plays a fundamental role in the field of study. The collectors themselves are sometimes among the best connoisseurs of their respective fields of interest and collaborate with important contributions to research, in the form of detailed studies or catalogs on the scientific progress of the subject. In the system of university education, numismatics is included among the auxiliary sciences of history and archeology and in particular it operates essentially in the field of the history of classical antiquities.

Numismatic classification

Numismatics does not only include the study of coins but encompasses a wide range of other fields, such as:

✓ Banknotes

✓ Other forms of money

✓ Medallions

✓ Medals

✓ Religious medals

✓ Tokens

So, after defining numismatics, let's see how it can be classified: usually, two macro-categories are taken into consideration, one relating to the Western tradition and the other to the Eastern one.

From a historical point of view, some great periods can be recognized in western numismatics:

✓ Ancient numismatics

✓ Greek coinage

✓ Autonomous coinage

✓ Royal coinage

✓ Ancient Italian coinage

✓ Roman coinage

✓ Roman republican coinage

✓ Imperial coinage

✓ Imperial coinage

✓ Provincial coinage

✓ Byzantine coinage

✓ Medieval coinage

✓ Modern coinage

✓ Contemporary coinage

For what about eastern tradition:

✓ Muslim coinage

✓ Indian coinage

✓ Chinese coinage

Numismatics Facts

Before concluding this brief chapter on numismatics, let us analyze some facts concerning it.

Let's start from a rather obvious fact: numismatics, as such, is not only a form of collecting but a real discipline, within which many other sectors converge and are linked. Money is a cultural product, one of the greatest human inventions that brought about a change in the social life of people. Since its inception, it has made its potential felt, above all as an economic tool: maximization of production and income, simplification and development of trade between populations, and reduction of transaction times and costs. In its social function, money has developed and perfected from generation to generation, such as navigation and writing, to such an extent that it has become an everyday and fundamental object. Its representative role should be remembered, with the numerous symbols and iconography that give life to the past of a nation, of a people, of a civilization, to its deepest and most radical history, and to its tradition.

Numismatists carry out a work of interpretation, through which tradition is brought back to life, what is hidden behind an illustration, writing, to put it briefly, behind a choice from the past. You dig deep to find what has been lost or forgotten, all with a strong desire, with work, study and will: only in this way being able to feed curiosity. The study of numismatics allows us to get to know humanity, its different cultures and customs over time, through analysis methods and techniques that demonstrate and determine the success of this constant research. Coins are an expression of art, civilization and the progress of peoples, they collect the past culture that the numismatist wants to preserve, since the past is not the past, it is not a closed chapter, but always open, still alive through the various research, analyses, documentation, conferences and more…

As the metal is shaped in the creation of a coin, the history and its conception are modified through continuous insights and studies, therefore numismatics plays and will always play a fundamental role, through its analytical, scrupulous and reflective method.

Another fact concerns the very origins of numismatics: the Greeks, and certainly the Romans, probably already had an interest in ancient coins and made them a collection item. It is a Roman historian of the 4th century, Flavio Vopisco, who leaves us the first example of the use of money as a document capable of contributing to the reconstruction of history: a concept that will later be very clear to Cassiodorus, the Roman statesman of the Ostrogoth Theodoric, who in 536 he made it the programmatic basis for the execution of coins. The Early Middle Ages marked a decline in the knowledge of ancient coins, in line with the lack of interest in classical culture.

A turning point towards a scientific approach to numismatic is impressed in the 14th century by the Italian poet. Petrarch, thanks to his knowledge of the classical texts, is led to make exact observations of a historical nature on the Roman coins of the empire. In the meantime, the great Italian and European collections were formed: princes, kings, and popes collected Greek and Roman coins. The possibility also arises of compiling the first books dedicated to iconography, in which the design of coins with portraits of famous people is accompanied by descriptive text. Particularly renowned are the works of the Roman scholar and collector F. Orsini, who also dedicates a volume to the coins of republican Rome (1577). The great fame of Orsini among his contemporaries is also linked to his ability to discern counterfeit coins. In the 16th century. the first signs of scholarly interest in medieval coins also appear. These, unlike the Greek and Roman series, have not found such early attention from collectors and scholars, perhaps due to their appearance, which often does not meet the aesthetic standards in vogue; but a not secondary role must have been played by the lack of interest in one's own local history, and therefore the ignorance of the events to which the coin was linked.

For periods in which there are few written sources, coins have a high value as sources both for the chronology and for the history of science, culture and the economy. This particularly applies to Greek and Roman antiquities, but also to areas outside the ancient Mediterranean cultures (e.g., for the Parthian and Scythian empires) as well as to the early and early Middle Ages.

For these periods, the monetary discoveries (that is, the coins that are found in a burial together with other objects or in some treasure) are important not only to facilitate dating but also as historical sources. A veritable numismatics of finds has developed, which currently constitutes the most dynamic and methodologically innovative part of this science.

Since the Middle Ages, with the increase in the frequency of written sources, numismatics is particularly linked to the history of money, to which it gives both historical and economic foundations. In more recent times, with the strong increase in the importance of coined money, numismatics becomes a staple in the history of the economy.

In addition to a highly specialized ancillary discipline of history and archaeology, numismatics also has numerous connections with neighboring disciplines such as economic history, social history, art history or onomastics. It is therefore one of the oldest forms of collecting, but still little-known today is undoubtedly the numismatic one.

As for other facts about numismatics, we can talk about the methods applied. in the strictest sense, they are essentially linked to the object money of. Other methodological principles derive from problems in the history of money.

Coins are a mass product, with the same shape, made in large numbers; however, every single coin, also due to the minting methods, is an individual with special characteristics (minting errors, variations in materials, irregularities).

The most important numismatic method, which serves to reconstruct the sequence of minting, is the analysis of the dies. It is based on the observation that each coin (two-sided) is made up of an anvil die (obverse) and a hammer die (reverse).

The two dies, which in hammered coinage are distinguished in upper die - or hammer dies - or lower die - and anvil die - wear out at different times. The hammer die must be replaced more frequently than the anvil dies. This leads to the so-called coinage combinations; the different combinations form a chain of dies which corresponds to the temporal sequence with which the single dies were produced and used. Coinage analysis was first used in the 19th century and introduced into Greek numismatics by Friedrich Imhoof-Blumer.

Other important methods for determining mutual chronology or contemporaneity are the study of the typology and the analysis of style. The limitations of these methods lie in the fact that only an infinitesimally small number of the originally minted coins have survived. Estimates based on coin discoveries suggest that today we have no more than one per thousand of the coins originally minted. Another important role is now also played by scientific research such as the analysis of metals, which gives indications on the origin of monetary metals but can also give answers to monetary policy problems (variations in the purity title of metals within the framework of a devaluation).

As the last fact, we can underline the "Find numismatics": it deals less with the single coin and more with groups of coins that make up the various categories of coin finds. It examines the distribution in the territory of the various types of coins keeping in mind the problems of the currency course, the history of the economy, traffic and commerce (market area, routes of goods and commerce).

With the facts on numismatics, we have concluded the third part of this guide. In the final part we will look at the reasons why it might be worth collecting coins, what are the pros and cons, and the types of coins that can be collected.

CHAPTER 4: COIN COLLECTION BASICS

In this final part of the guide, we are going to see what the reasons, advantages and disadvantages are of collecting coins, without forgetting what are the types of coins that you can collect.

Why Coin Collecting?

So, let's briefly see the reasons why to start now collect coins.

So why do we collect, and why does numismatics continue to exist after all these centuries? Evidently, there is something that makes it stand and this thing can be identified with the spirit of investigation, curiosity, knowledge and above all love for history, culture and art. Numismatics is always at hand, literally, a hand that touches the past and analyzes it, together with the mind's eye that studies it. The collaboration and mutual exchange of precious information, typical of numismatists, allows and will increasingly allow us to clarify and reveal what the past has to tell us, a continuous search toward the truth. Another reason why it would be better to collect coins instead of banknotes, for example, is wear and tear and durability. Banknotes, in fact, are easily subject to wear due to the fragility of the paper, it is, therefore, essential to know how to handle and store them properly, in order to avoid causing folds, undulations, stains, etc... You need to have, to be clear, a fairy hand. While the coins are made, precisely to last over time, to resist and, with some tricks to avoid wear.

Another reason could be a reason for enriching historical and cultural knowledge. In fact, historical coins of which very few written forms have survived represent a high scientific, historical, geographical and economic value, especially those belonging to the Roman, Greek, Mediterranean, Early Middle Ages and Early Middle Ages. Numismatics in this case assumes the term "discovery", to indicate precisely the discovery of the coins of these peoples buried together with other objects or burials.

Another reason is precisely linked to the historical value of the coin itself. Since its origins, the currency has stylistically reflected the cultural and economic characteristics of the various regions to which it belongs and, over the centuries, has remained intimately linked to its history. In fact, unlike any other kind of artifact, it has always maintained the connotation of official art and therefore the utmost respect for the cultural and religious tradition of society; moreover, when, starting from the Roman Empire, contemporary events began to be depicted, in addition to the portraits of the emperors, the coin also took on clear political purposes.

Another important reason to start collecting coins is purely recreational: think of a completely healthy hobby, against stress that allows you to use your time in a functional way. Also, think about the fact of starting a new hobby that can involve parents-kids.In fact, coin collecting could very well be a reason to bond families or to make a legal, educational and exemplary activity for your children.

What Can You Collect?

Different collectible types of coins

The different characteristics of each coinage can provide a wide choice, satisfying any type of cultural and aesthetic orientation.

Greek numismatics is divided into continental and colonial. The colonial one, especially the coinage of Magna Graecia and Sicily, is undoubtedly the most refined from a stylistic point of view, the most sought after in the world and collected, together with the Roman one, since before the eighteenth century throughout Europe.

The coinage of the Roman period is extremely interesting in terms of the variety of mythological themes and the iconographic panorama: from Caesar onwards, portraits of all the great personalities of the time, the emperors and the great socio-political figures of the time are depicted.

The coinage of the Byzantine and barbarian periods is interesting for the stylistic peculiarities and for the entry of Christianity into religious themes, while the numismatics of the early Middle Ages undoubtedly reflects the darkness of that historical period and, at the same time, the charm and mystery that surround it.

The coins of the following periods chronologically express the cultural and artistic vitality of the Renaissance, the opulence of the Baroque, and the rigor and industrial evolution of the modern age. The Renaissance period is undoubtedly the most prestigious: the coin recovers the very high artistic level which had declined with the end of the Roman Empire and in Italy, the affirmation of powerful lordships such as those of the Gonzaga, the Este, the Farnese, the Sforza and dei Medici, gives life to one of the most beautiful and interesting coins in the world.

If you want to buy gold coins, it is good to rely on safe and certified coins. First of all, sovereign coins, i.e. those issued by states.

- American Eagle (United States): characterized by the very famous image of the eagle symbol of America, it is the most significant investment coin of the United States of America. It has a face value of $50 and is considered one of the best investment gold coins.
- Maple Leaf (Canada): by far one of the most traded investment coins on the market, it is distinguished by the characteristic maple leaf, a symbol of Canada. On the market, it is recognized as one of the most beautiful and prestigious gold coins, also because it was practically the first to be minted with a purity of 99.9%, therefore at 24 carats.

- Kangaroo (Australia): also called Nugget (nugget), from 1986 and until 1989 it really represented a nugget. In subsequent issues, a red kangaroo was instead depicted, considered more representative of the country. Made in 24 carats, it is distinguished by its limited edition and the fact that it is minted every year with a new motif.

- Philharmonic (Austria): issued for the first time in 1989, it is absolutely one of the best-selling and most appreciated investment coins in the world. It was the first coin of its kind to be issued with a face value in euros, while until 2002 it was minted in shillings.

- Panda (China): each year the design of these coins is renewed, which increases the numismatic value. This makes this bullion coin a favorite with collectors, as well as investors of course.

- Gold Sovereign (England): Gold Sovereign, the real name of this well-known gold coin, is to be considered absolutely one of the best investment coins on the market thanks to its history and obviously the prestige of the issuing country.

- Marengo (Italy): it was issued for the first time in 1801 to celebrate the French victory over the Austrians of the previous year and for this reason, it is also called Napoleon. With regard to the issues of the Italian state, it was minted from 1861 to 1923, but not continuously, which makes it a coin with a strong numismatic value. In principle, the medieval and Renaissance coins are the most valuable.

Other kinds of collecting coins are:

Commemorative: coins that celebrate or indeed commemorate a certain historical period, like those indicated above. There are several reasons to purchase a commemorative coin or series of coins:

a) We can keep them as a souvenir, or reminder of an event and/or place visited.

b) By virtue of their admirable design and pattern they can become splendid ornamental objects.

c) They can be an original way to give a gift, an increasing practice both between people and within companies.

d) It is a noble experience to own a collection of these types of coins, as they are objects of interest, of remarkable beauty, value and sometimes a rarity.

e) We can consider it a sort of investment, as they acquire value over time. This revaluation factor makes them an asset that deserves to be preserved.

In addition to coins in normal circulation, there are other types:

✓ Bullion Coins. The concept of "Bullion" is that of a coin minted in precious metal, the value of which is not fixed by the value stamped on the coin, but by the value of the metal it is made of. The need for this type of coin arises when the price of the metal becomes unstable, and the value begins to fluctuate, and it becomes convenient to invest in raw metal for speculative purposes. Many investors prefer the metal in coin form over other forms such as bars, bars, etc., as coins do not need to be analyzed before being offered for sale. Many Governments, faced with the demand from the investing public, mint these coins, not for the common legal tender of circulation, but to be specifically sold as "bullion". Basically, they are coins minted in precious metal (gold and silver), on the occasion of sporting, political or cultural events. Generally, this type of coin has great beauty in its motifs and designs and brings together the aspect of the Proof coin, the medal and the coin of common circulation. It becomes an authentic collector's item and is not placed on the market as a normal bargaining chip. This coin, or series of coins, is minted in a limited number of copies. They are generally presented in transparent plastic packages, or in special paper or wooden binders.

✓ Circulating: coins that are still in circulation
✓ Uncirculated: coins that are no longer used for commercial exchanges and that belong to different eras.
✓ Medals of certain historical and cultural error coins.

Pro And Cons of Coin Collecting as A Business

Let's see, in this final chapter, what are the advantages and disadvantages of considering coin collecting with a real business.

Pros

The main advantage is the convenience of storing coins that can be kept at home, possibly in a safe. If you then want to resell them because perhaps the price of the metal increases, it is certainly more immediate to sell them than ingots. Another advantage is the high liquidity of the coin, accepted by any retailer and also by banking institutions without particular problems, as coins that have been minted by governments are reliable and safe. Conversely, reselling an ingot requires an authenticity test to determine the quality of the metal. Investment coins are therefore cashier easier and faster. Possibility of savings. As for collector coins, they are regularly quoted based on the real-time quotations of the metals they are made of. But their most important feature is that they have a value that revalues over time, with not excessive upward or downward fluctuations. The possibilities of loss are reduced to a minimum, while the possibilities of gain are manifold because they essentially depend on the possibilities of increase in value that these coins have in the eyes of collectors and on the prices that are beaten at auctions to win them. Investing in collectible coins can be done by buying gold, silver, bronze coins, or a mix of coins of different materials, to diversify your investment. Numismatics is the only pleasure item that goes from Ancient Greece to the present day, giving collectors the opportunity for a real journey through time. There are several interesting aspects of buying ancient coins. First of all, it is a free investment. In fact, a collection can be set up according to one's own taste and availability, freeing oneself from purely economic logic. The obsessive search for quality, in this sense, often becomes a negative element, which precludes the emotional return.

Another final advantage is that an investment is accessible to all: the same coin can be purchased for hundreds of euros or tens of thousands of euros depending on the condition. Finally, numismatics, above all culture. By purchasing a vintage coin, you can hold the history of our civilization in your hands, and this is the most important value.

Cons

Authenticity. As in other forms of collecting, it is important to proceed with caution, turning to qualified and well-known dealers: unfortunately, numismatics too is afflicted by the problem of forgeries and only the decennial experience of an expert professional can give guarantees of authenticity. It is also very important to have the guarantee that what you buy has a legal origin, a guarantee that only qualified traders can give.

When choosing suppliers, it is, therefore, preferable to contact traders registered with trade associations.

It is not always as easy as it might seem: the aspiring collector, after having established the subject of his interest, must deepen his knowledge of the subject by examining the coins live, in numismatic studios and shops, or by requesting auction catalogs and price lists sale to specialized houses, to know and understand the stylistic peculiarities and the differences of the various degrees of conservation and evaluation of the material offered. The first purchases must not be of particularly valuable or rare pieces, but of representative and stimulating coins for the continuation of the collection; it is also essential to buy books for the classification and study of them.

BOOK 2: DETERMINE COINS VALUE

Introduction

With the first guide, we dealt with describing the anatomy of coins, numismatics and the pros and cons of coin collecting itself. Now that we have quite clear ideas and want to start collecting coins, both as a hobby and to create a real business, the time has come to deepen our knowledge.

We have now understood that coin collecting is a form of collecting and trading that involves coins or other forms of legally issued currency.

We have also seen that numismatics can be a hobby but also a way to invest or earn money quickly. In fact, collecting ancient or rare coins can also lead to very high earnings and the investment can be long or short-term. It is therefore something perfectly legitimate and positive which often has many advantages and can actually represent a form of income.

As regards the possible types of coins, already described in the first guide, we have seen that coin collecting includes those coins which have circulated for short periods, minted with errors, or are considered particularly beautiful, or have particular historical and cultural significance.

Now it's time to start distinguishing the various coins, their value and if they are worth adding to our collection. Having said that, here we are again to help you with this second guide: in fact, you will be shown what are all the necessary parameters and aspects to recognize and evaluate the quality of the coins we would like to collect.

But that's not all: you will have a series of practical tips that will help you distinguish fake coins from originals.

Specifically, this guide will be divided into 5 main parts:

✓ In the first part of this second guide, we will explain all the factors that experts study to value a coin. So, we will understand what gives coin value.

✓ In the second part, we will underline deeper coin value and show you all the features of coin grading. Having understood the quality and value of the coin (as we will see also from the professional expert opinion) we will be able to see if our coin is worthy of collecting or not.

✓ Moving on into the third part, we will explain step by step how to identify a coin, and where to find its value of that coin.

✓ In the fourth part, all about business, we will indicate all the tips to send you coin collection.

✓ In the fifth and last part of this guide, we will deal with the history of counterfeited coins and how to identify fake, with specific differentiation details for gold coins, silver coins, and so on…

At the end of reading this second guide, you will understand how to evaluate, and have your coin collection evaluated, how to sell it to an excellent bidder and make money, but also how to distinguish the value of the coins based on the materials used to make them.

CHAPTER 1: WHAT GIVES COINS VALUE?

In this first chapter and part of the book, we will analyze all the factors that experts study to value a coin. Understanding the value of our coins is really important in case we have to sell and know how much we could do it.

Coins or money value: what is?

Before understanding the factors considered by experts to understand the value of a coin, let's analyze for a moment the concept of the value of the coin itself.

We have already been able to ascertain, from the first book, that money (not understood as currency but as a general concept) is a cultural product that we have used for millennia to regulate the exchange of goods and services between us human beings. This cultural product can manifest itself in time and space under the most diverse forms: it can be a metal object, a coin, a sheet of paper, a shell, a medallion or a simple number on a spreadsheet. To give a precise definition, we can say that the value or purchasing power of money means the number of goods and services that can be purchased with it. But money can take on very different meanings in relation to its value.

Money is above all a means of exchange, i.e., the instrument through which to acquire a good or a service: for example, when we go to the market, we exchange our coins and banknotes at the cash desk for a certain quantity of fruit and vegetables.

At the same time, money is a measure of value; in fact, it allows us to assign a precise quantitative value to each good or service, or object of exchange.

But, the value of each coin, and this seems rather obvious to us, is the one marked on the coin itself. The value of a coin on the basis of the current market remains, regardless of its rarity, always and only nominal. And, therefore, a 1-euro coin will always have the value of one euro if used for buying and selling. The value of a rare coin is given by the secondary market, that of numismatists and collectors who, precisely because of the desire to own rare pieces, determine the increase in prices at least for the specimens auctioned.

But, it is essential in modern economies to have means of payment in the quantity necessary to regulate ever-increasing flows of exchanges.

This implies that the monetary authorities have the freedom to issue money in the amount they deem adequate for the proper functioning of the payment system. The currency is not issued against gold reserves held by the central bank, as was the case in the past, nor can it, therefore, be sold to the issuing bank in exchange for gold or another asset.

The circulation of money and therefore the recognition of its nominal value depends only on the trust that whoever receives a certain amount of money in payment can in turn transfer this money to other subjects in exchange for other goods and services. This "fiduciary mechanism" guarantees that the nominal value is also the real value of the coin.

Naturally, all the anti-counterfeiting systems intervene to strengthen this mechanism based on mutual trust, which offers citizens a high probability that the money owned (and received from others) will be recognized at the nominal value shown on banknotes and coins and not the intrinsic value of banknotes and coins. These coins do have not any legal value.

Therefore, a first factor that must absolutely be taken into consideration with regard to coin collecting is that the latter are not counterfeit. A counterfeit coin has no value, so besides not being able to be resold, it doesn't even deserve to be in our personal collection.

In the last chapter of this guide, we will examine the concept of counterfeiting even better and avoid its unpleasant drawbacks.

What are the parameters used by experts to establish the value of a coin?

After describing what the value of the coin is, let's see what factors are taken into consideration by the experts to determine the value of a coin. As we have seen just above, we can attribute different meanings to the term value of money, depending on the perspective from which we analyze this particular human invention; Consequently, one can speak of:

✓ Legal or nominal value: the value attributed to the currency by the laws of the State which regulate its issue and circulation; it is the value that the coin bears printed, it is recognized by all and is not subject to variations.

✓ Real value: the purchasing power of money (i.e., the number of goods and services that can be purchased at a given time with the use of money).

✓ The intrinsic value is the value of the coin considered as metal. It corresponds to the value of the quantity of more or less precious metals of which it is formed. However, this value only concerns metal money, since paper money, as everyone knows, has a low intrinsic value (only paper, color, design and printing). The intrinsic value of a coin, in other words, is the value of the instrument (for example, the metal coin or the bank note) used as money. It depends on the value of the asset that makes up the currency. A paper currency, such as a $10 bill, has an intrinsic value equal to the cost of producing it, i.e., the cost of inks, printing, transportation from the printing house to the bank, anti-counterfeiting fees, etc. Similarly, a metal coin, such as the $1 coin, has an intrinsic value equal to the cost to mint it. The intrinsic value of the instrument never exceeds the nominal value, to avoid a negative seigniorage, a cost of production of the coin greater than the revenue that is obtained by spending it, and because the users would have the incentive to melt them down to recover the metal, or to use them for a purpose other than exchange. So, the intrinsic value of the coin is subject to change as the price of the metal changes. The quantity of precious metal that can be extracted is not correlated to the wealth produced, nor is a country rich because it has many reserves, or is necessarily obliged to keep them in proportion to its economic growth. The absence of a reserve obligation, to avoid abuses in the issuance of money, is compensated by a governance system that entrusts the coinage to independent authorities, who have the task of regulating it in order to avoid inflation. These are usually modest costs. The intrinsic value of modern coins is therefore very low, with the exception of coins that assume a numismatic interest for which the intrinsic value remains low, but the rarity, the desire to collect them and all that feeds the interest of numismatists contributes to give them a value. The gradual transition from the use of coins in precious metals to immaterial coins has reduced the intrinsic value of the coin and consequently also the costs to produce it. The reduction in costs occurred at the same time as the growth of the economy which made it necessary to use ever larger quantities of money.

But, in addition to these purely economic factors, there are many other factors that can determine the value of a coin. First of all, the date the coin was minted.

It should be noted that even if ancient coins can have a very high value, in this specific field the axiom the older the more valuable is not always to be considered essential. In fact, some euro coins minted after 2000 can be worth more than lira coins from the 1950s. Because collectors' interest in a coin is not determined solely by how old it is.

In any case, when we are speaking in particular of the value of collector's coins, a factor that predominates is certainly, in addition to the metals used, the rarity: although it may seem a paradox, in fact, as collector's items also those that we commonly call "money" have a price, and directly proportional to their rarity.

In fact, the value of the coin is mainly determined by its rarity: in fact, if millions of coins have been minted of the same specimen, it will be very difficult for it to reach significant values.

If the antiquity of a coin is added to the rarity, it is easy to understand that: if a 1900 coin was produced in 1 million specimens, there are most likely many in circulation among collectors; if a coin also from 1900 was minted in only 100 specimens, very probably very few have arrived today and those few have an immense value.

Furthermore, the rarity of a coin is also measured in other factors, and not only in how many specimens it was minted. A coin can be defined as rare even if it is proof, i.e. minted before the specimen defined to test it: proof coins are usually used to test the molds and for this reason, a very limited quantity is produced.

A coin can be rare even if its design is changed during its production or if the composition of the material changes: an example can be the 1943 Lincoln penny which was initially minted in steel due to the scarcity of copper (in full Second World War). In other cases, the coins were initially minted in silver and later replaced by other materials such as copper or nickel when the precious metal underwent a surge in price.

Coins can become rare even when they are withdrawn if produced by mistake or with errors (an example could be given by the 500 Italian lire in silver with the Caravelle whose first trial edition is worth a fortune also due to the minting error).

An impact on the value of the currency can also be given by the country that issued it. Not all countries, however, show their name on the coins they issue, and if there is, it could also be written in Latin or in the language of the country itself (think of countries, for example, that use alphabets other than Latin...). To know the country where the coin was minted, if you can't figure it out, you can do an online search.

Finally, the state of conservation is decisive for the value of the coin. The better the coin is kept, the more its value rises; the coins with a higher value are those " Uncirculated", i.e., those that have never circulated and are brand new (as if just minted). If a coin shows signs of wear due to circulation (scratches, corrosion of the images, etc...) its market value is bound to be lower than the estimates you can find in numismatic catalogs since those almost always refer to the coin in perfect condition. storage conditions.

Now that we have understood what are the main factors that determine the value of a coin, in the next chapter, we will deepen the discussion by talking about coin grading.

CHAPTER 2: DETERMINE COIN MARKET VALUE WITH GRADING

In this second part of the guide, we will analyze the coin grading, the quality of the coins and who are the experts able to correctly evaluate the value of our collectible coins.

Understanding Coin Grading

Collecting coins, which has always been defined as «the hobby of kings» from how it was deduced from the first guide, is also called "numismatics", but improperly because numismatics is like we have seen in more detail, the in-depth study of the coin and its history.

Now, when it comes to coin collecting, the concept of grading cannot be ignored. In fact, classifying coins is essential in order to establish the parameters indicated in the previous chapter and understand their possible value.

Their evaluation basically depends on their rarity and their state of conservation, the fact that they can also be of precious metal is just another parameter to consider (they will always have a value for the pure gold contained).

Coin grading is nothing more than those set of standards that are used to determine whether a coin is worth a lot or not. Among these standards we have:

✓ Degrees of conservation - Conservation is fundamental to establishing the value of the coin. How many degrees are there?

✓ Rarity Grades - The higher the Rarity the higher the value of the coin.

✓ Metal acronyms - There are many metals used in numismatics, let's learn to identify them.

✓ Technical terms - Consulting Italian and foreign catalogs and price lists, it is easy to come across little-known technical terms.

So, let's see how these two standards are codified:

Degrees of rarity

✓ VC = very common

✓ C = common

✓ UC = uncommon

✓ R = rare

✓ R2 = very rare

- ✓ R3 = very much rare
- ✓ R4 = extremely rare
- ✓ R5 = few specimens

U = unique

A coin can be rare, but not particularly sought after on the market, just as antiquity by itself does not give the coin great value.

Degrees of conservation

- ✓ (VG = very good): the coin is almost completely worn
- ✓ (F = fine): clearly visible wear
- ✓ (VF = very fine): slight traces of wear
- ✓ (EF = extremely fine): almost without traces of wear
- ✓ (UNC = uncirculated): perfect condition as it has never been circulated.

From this, it is clear that even small differences in conservation can lead to large differences in value. But there is still a higher level of classification, and they are the coins that are called "proof".

They are coins issued in an extremely limited edition and, above all, worked with great care (with a mirrored back) which are usually put up for sale in prestigious boxes. The first known proof coins were minted in silver in 1662 in England, at first only on special occasions such as the accession to the throne of a new ruler, then it became customary to use them as gifts for important foreign personalities and finally, nowadays, they are issued from all the mints of the world with the sole purpose of raising cash.

Quality of Coins

When we look at coins for the first time, they all seem to be in excellent condition. In reality, as we gain experience, we realize that we have coins in our collection with different degrees of wear. Since the value of coins is also given by their state of conservation, it is important to know how they can be classified.

The state of conservation of a coin has always been the subject of controversy between collectors, operators in the sector and enthusiasts. The difficulty in attributing a precise quality to a specimen is a difficult undertaking: we have deemed it useful to codify a classification method that can answer the perplexities of many, above all those who do not have a great experience and offer a simple and immediate answer to those working in this difficult field.

We have taken a system linked to the already existing states of conservation, BB, SPL, and FDC, with a numerical and progressive linear formula that divides each quality level into ten parts, and allows us to attribute a conservation value with a deviation of one-tenth per time.

The Sheldon coin grading and European system

These two types of scale can be considered conservation states

The state of conservation of the coins is regulated by convention by various degrees, indicated by a scale that must be applied with scruple and professionalism. In a project that I believe offers the greatest possible flexibility, we have included seven degrees of conservation, the same considered in the previous paragraph. To deeper this discussion we could say that the Sheldon scale takes into consideration the state of conservation of coins as the main element capable of classifying their value. The Sheldon scale is a 70-point scale that ranks coins by condition on a juncture ranging from mediocre/poor (P-1) to perfect mint condition (MS-70). In fact, a poor or mediocre coin (P-1) must have a date and a mint mark visible if used but identifying it is really difficult due to the damage it has suffered. On the contrary, instead a coin in a perfect state of conservation and therefore mint (MS-70) is impeccable, even if it were to be looked at under a microscope. The design is centered and the shot is very crisp and clear. It must be said, however, that only uncirculated coins fall into this category because coins undergo wear when they are used and touched, and the more often they are, the more they will have a poorer state of conservation.

So, we have:

from the lowest rank:

✓ P = Poor

Modest state of conservation, to be attributed to a very worn coin with unreadable parts of the legends and undefined contours. Not collectible, except for rarity.

✓ F = Fair

A little more than the modest state of conservation, not used in collectors' manuals, nor in public auctions, a category that indicates a worn and worn coin with recognizable reliefs and evident traces of wear, without prejudice to the degree of rarity and the value of the intrinsic content.

✓ VF = Very Fair

Degree of conservation not in use, indicating a little sought-after quality, for a very worn coin with legible reliefs but generally not pleasant to look at: also in this case the value lies in the rarity and in the intrinsic content.

✓ G = Good

It is in an almost pleasant state of conservation, with wear percentages around fifty percent of the new coin; even in this quality, except for rarities, even the most modest, the value is given by the intrinsic content.

✓ VG = Very Good

It is a pleasant coin with signs of wear that must not exceed thirty percent of the new coin. This is the first state of conservation in which a coin begins to have a higher value than its intrinsic value, even if it were not rare.

✓ SPL = Gorgeous

Indicates a state of conservation already highly sought after especially for small and large rarities; this quality represents a coin that has circulated very little and still retains the reflections of the minting with intact reliefs and traces of wear that must not exceed ten percent of the new coin. In this state of conservation, even the most common coins take on a value many times higher than their intrinsic value.

✓ UB or mint state = Brilliant Uncirculated

It has no signs of wear; highly sought after for its quality, this conservation is very rare even for very common specimens, the coin retains the freshness of the newly minted specimen, and its value rises greatly compared to the same specimens of different quality.

✓ OTS = Outstanding

The currency that constitutes an exception, with respect to a norm that it derogates in a superlative, extraordinary or formidable sense. The Exceptional specimen has no traces of wear or signs of contact, or minting taps but is characterized by a state of exception. In this case, the value is for specialists or amateurs. it is a clean coin.

✓ Very rare specimen

This applies to all levels of rarity. Of course, even in this case, there is an exception because a very rare specimen in an even lower state of conservation can be considered an Exceptional coin.

Here is a scale that includes the European system instead, with the best condition being on the left:

ITALIA	FDC	SPL	BB	MB	B
U.S.A.	UNC	EF	VF	F	VG
UK	UNC	EF	VF	F	VG
Germany	STG	VZ	SS	S	SGE
France	FDC	SUP	TTB	TB	BC
Spain	SC	EBC	MBC	BC	RC
Portugal	SOB	BELA	MBC	BC	MREG
Holland	FDC	PR	ZF	FR	ZG
Baltic Countries	0	01	1+	1	1-

Classification of coins in Classes of Minting

There is also a further method of coin classification that goes beyond the usual classifications listed above, called "Giant" and used by the Catalog of Italian coins published by Fabio Gigante. The editor says verbatim:

".... not all coins, as many think, are easily available, regardless of their degree of conservation, in perfect minting conditions: tired dies, minting scratches, flattening, contours with poorly engraved mottos or disfiguring the edge, etc. ..they are in many cases, generally found and in others, they constitute the rule....."

The subdivision of the coins according to this method is organized into 3 classes, namely:

1. 1ST CLASS: Coins without minting defects. (The presence of defects decreases the value).
2. 2nd CLASS: Coins generally with minting defects. (The absence of defects increases the value).
3. 3RD CLASS: Coins almost always with minting defects. (The absence of defects increases the value more).

Metal acronyms

Let's see together the acronyms of the metals used to understand the quality of the coin.

- ✓ Ac - Acmonital
- ✓ Ae - Bronze
- ✓ Ag - Silver
- ✓ Al - Aluminum
- ✓ Au - Gold
- ✓ Ba - Bronzital
- ✓ Cn - Copper/Nickel
- ✓ Cu - Copper
- ✓ El - Electro
- ✓ Fe - Iron
- ✓ It - Italma
- ✓ Nb - Niobium
- ✓ Ni - Nickel
- ✓ Pl - palladium
- ✓ Pt - Platinum
- ✓ Zn - Zinc

Technical terms

Now let's see some basic technical terms to understand the quality of the coin.

Consulting foreign catalogs and price lists, it is easy to come across technical terms, sometimes little known and of which we may not know the meaning perfectly. Below, we will list the most common ones in alphabetical order.

- ✓ Area - see Field.
- ✓ Double beating - Deburring of the minting due to the movement of the coin during minting.
- ✓ Very beautiful - State of conservation (see degrees of conservation).
- ✓ Beautiful - State of conservation (see degrees of conservation).
- ✓ Billon - Type of alloy (see metal codes).
- ✓ Brilliant - The type of processing makes the treated part shiny.
- ✓ Brillant Uncirculated - English term meaning Brilliant uncirculated (used by the English mint).
- ✓ Bullion - English term meaning stock exchange coins.
- ✓ Field - Space between the type and the legend or the edge of the coin.
- ✓ Carat - Percentage of gold in a coin relative to its weight. 1 carat equals 1/24 of the total weight.
- ✓ Conservation - State in which the coin is currently found.
- ✓ Worn - Worn, poorly preserved.
- ✓ Outline - Thickness of the coin.
- ✓ Countermark - Letter or symbol which, added later on the coin, modifies its value.
- ✓ Date - Year of minting of the coin.
- ✓ Right - In numismatics we mean the part that corresponds to the observer's right.
- ✓ Obverse - Main face of the coin.
- ✓ Straight - see Straight.
- ✓ Epigraph - see Legend.
- ✓ Exergue - Low field of the coin, under the representation of the central field.
- ✓ Face - Side of the coin (obverse or reverse).
- ✓ Brilliant Uncirculated - State of conservation (see degrees of conservation).
- ✓ Proof - The type of processing makes the bottom of the coin mirror.
- ✓ Giro - Part of the coin near the edge where the legend is written.
- ✓ Knurling - See knurling.
- ✓ Footprint - The set of type and legend.
- ✓ Incuses - That which is lower than the field surface in the footprint.
- ✓ Legend - Inscription on the coin.
- ✓ Retrograde Legend - Legend wrote from right to left.
- ✓ Thousandths - Percentage of precious metal in a coin compared to its weight.
- ✓ Matte proof - English term meaning satin.

- ✓ Millennial - Date of minting of a coin or series of coins.
- ✓ Mint - English term meaning Mint.
- ✓ Mintage - English term meaning Print run.
- ✓ Module - Diameter of the coin.
- ✓ Very beautiful - State of conservation (see degrees of conservation).
- ✓ Monogram - Set of connected letters.
- ✓ Nummi – Coins.
- ✓ Rim - Extreme part of the edge of the coin.
- ✓ Oxidation - Natural process of the metal in contact with oxygen or with oxidizing agents in general.
- ✓ Patina Film forms on the coin as a result of the metal oxidation process.
- ✓ Proof - English term meaning Proof.
- ✓ Proof-like - English term which means glossy or brilliant workmanship.
- ✓ Reverse - Side of the coin opposite the obverse.
- ✓ Sandblasted - see satin.
- ✓ Satin - The type of processing makes the treated part opaque.
- ✓ Mint mark - Initial or design indicating the mint of the issue of the coin.
- ✓ Splendid - State of conservation (see degrees of conservation).
- ✓ Cut - See cont.
- ✓ Type - The main figure or object depicted on the coin.
- ✓ Circulation - Quantity of coins issued (relative to the same date, mint...).
- ✓ Fineness - Percentage of metal, precious or not, of which a coin must be composed.
- ✓ Tolerance - Allowable margin of error for the weight and/or fineness of a coin.
- ✓ Flan - The metal disc that forms the coin.
- ✓ Intrinsic Value - The only value of the metal contained in the coin.
- ✓ Face value - Legal value affixed to the coin by the mint at the time of issue.
- ✓ Numismatic value - An added value of the coin beyond its intrinsic and nominal value.
- ✓ Mint - Place where coins are minted.
- ✓ Knurling - A series of parallel, vertical or oblique lines engraved around the edge of the coin.

Who can valuate my coin professionally?

Before starting to indicate who can help you understand the real value of the coins, let's make a small difference, which is the one that concerns investment coins and numismatic coins

Investment coins are those commonly classified as "bullion".

They are very common and are valid in practice for the pure metal contained. But it is said that then, for some reason, becoming difficult to find on the market, they cannot become coins with a numismatic value. Bullion coins are VAT exempt.

A different matter concerns numismatic coins. In this case, it happens that if the market demand (law of supply and demand) gives a coin a much higher value than that of the pure gold contained, this enters the category of numismatic coins and, by law, they are burdened with the 'VAT.

One might wonder if it might be worth buying a numismatic coin, certainly, These kinds of coins are those normally sought after by collectors for whom the price takes a back seat, but also if you want to limit yourself to considering the cost, you certainly over time this coin is destined to increase its value even more and therefore it would certainly be a good deal to own it.

And in any case, buying a gold coin, whatever it is, is a way to always secure your capital. In addition to the pleasure of owning a piece of history.

As for who can now evaluate your coins, we are talking about two subjects: PCGS and NGC.

PCGS or Professional Coin Grading Service was founded in 1985 in Santa Ana, California. Today, it is one of the world's leading services for sorting, attributing, authenticating and encapsulating coins. The founders of the company, including the President, David Hall and co-founder Silvano DeGenova, aimed to standardize the classification. Today, the company offers affordable, unbiased classification and authentication by the best experts in the industry. Many of the PCGS-certified coins have sold at higher prices at auctions in the past. PCGS now has subsidiaries in Europe, China and Asia and the company has so far graded over 33 million bullion coins.

PCGS certification is now the industry standard for third-party coin certification. It is a universal grading standard that allows all numismatic enthusiasts to buy and sell pieces without worrying about their authenticity and the physical condition of the coin. Numismatic experts working for PCGS are able to recognize and certify coins from the sixteenth century belonging to the currencies of over 100 countries, such as Australia, Brazil, Canada, China, France, Germany, Great Britain, Greece, Hong Kong, India, Italy, Japan, Mexico, New Zealand, Philippines, Poland, Russia, Singapore, Spain, Switzerland, United States, plus numerous African nations. PCGS has been in operation since 1986 and in nearly thirty years has graded 23 million coins for a worth of nearly $26 billion. The PCGS certificate manages to respond to a need that the world of numismatics has felt since the early twentieth century, and which mainly concerned the non-certain but subjective criteria with which coins were classified based on their conservation. In 1948 it was introduced the Sheldon Grading Scale, but even that failed to satisfy the need for a safe, universal standard. Sheldon's 1-70 scale is however the basis for the grading standard used by PCGS, which offers a complete description of each grade, with suffixes and no-grade codes. For example, VG-8 means "Worn Design with Slight Detail," while MS-PR-62 stands for "No Wear. Slightly less marked markings/engravings, the impression may not be complete", or again VF-20 stands for "Some details defined, all letters complete and clear". You can go to the PCGS website to see comparisons with other European conservation standards and make the necessary conversions.

NGC (Numismatic Guaranty Corporation) instead, is the largest privately owned international coin certification service, headquartered in Sarasota, Florida. Since its foundation in 1987, to date, NGC has certified almost 40 million coins, offering a unique service for collectors from all over the world. NGC certification consists of authentication, classification, attribution and encapsulation in transparent plastic holders of coins, medals and tokens.

For being more specific, this company has announced that it has certified over 50 million coins, tokens and medals, making it the first independent grading service to reach this impressive milestone. Fifty million coins which, reads a note, very often represent authentic numismatic rarities from the dawn of coinage to the present day, some recovered from the depths of the ocean and others that have even been taken to the moon.

NGC is a member of the Certified Collectibles Group (CCG), which owns five collectible certification services. NGC has been the official grading service of the American Numismatic Association (ANA) since 1995 and of the Professional Numismatists Guild (PNG) since 2004. The NGC corporate team consists of over 30 full-time graders and complete impartiality and objectivity are guaranteed: in fact, NGC classifiers are prohibited from trading coins, precisely in the face of impartiality.

Should I have my Coin graded?

Now that we know who the subjects are who can ensure that your coins can be certified and therefore have a value, if you think it is appropriate to have a coin that meets the indicated standards evaluated, contact these two companies.

As you might have guessed, grading is a long process and the cost depends on the coin's value, so you don't need to grade your coins always, and above all, grading is not a process you do when you have not yet identified your currency. Don't make this beginner mistake, so when you should grade your coin?

Grade your coin will cost you around 25$ if your coin is worth less than 300$ and can go up to 80$ excluding shipping and insurance (from 20 to 150$ depending on your coin's value). In terms of time, grading a coin can take from 1 to 6 months on regular basis and you can pay an extra fee for an express service. So, if your coin costs less than 300$ we recommend you not to do it. Obviously, the last decision is yours

If you just believe that you have a rare coin, but you are not sure, visit a coin dealer first to identify and confirm the rarity and authenticity. He will then identify the piece for you for free and if it is a valuable coin you can make the decision of grading.

CHAPTER 3: WHAT'S MY COIN WORTH?

In this short chapter, we will deal with explaining how to identify a collector's coin and where to find this coin's value.

How to identify a coin?

There is a practical format to identify your coin that will make it easier for you to catalog and find the value of your coin.

Year & Mint Mark, Type, Grade (optional)

In this format you find:

✓ Date: you should check along with face value. This is the simplest way that will help you to identify an old coin. For making some examples, you should know that Spanish coins minted since the early 17th century are those that can be considered among the oldest to have a date. Therefore, many old coins minted since that time, have been circulated enough to cause their dates to wear away. But, another thing very important to know is that some dates are listed using different calendar systems. For making another example, most parts of Moroccan coins have the Islamic calendar; Nepali coins are referred the Vikram Samvat calendar.

- ✓ Mint Mark: this is a letter or group of letters that indicate information about the city, state, or country where a coin was minted. You can find the mint mark on the coin reverse.

  For making an example, current American coins hold up the mint marks P (Philadelphia), D (Denver), S (San Francisco), or W (West Point). Other mint marks, for coins that were minted during the 19th century, include the letters C (Charlotte), and O (for New Orleans). In the case our coin has no mint mark, it was likely minted in Philadelphia, because no mint mark was used until World War II, and then appears again until 1968.

- ✓ Type: The inscription, or legend, insert in a coin can really be helpful to identify the type of coin and its country of mint and may also help determine its age if the date is missing.

  For making example, American coins usually declare "United States of America" somewhere on the coin you have found. You can also usually find the word "Liberty" and the mottoes "E Pluribus Unum" ("out of many, one") and "In God We Trust" (this was first used in 1863, and then on all coins after 1938). Another example could be older British coins. They generally have the Latin "Britannia" or some variation of it such as "Britannia" or "Britanniarum in their coins." Coins minted prior to 1953 commemorating the rule of a particular monarch may have "BRITT:OMN: REX," too which is short for the Latin phrase meaning "King (or Queen) of all Britons."

- ✓ Grade (we have already explained)

Let's make an example:

1981D, Penny or 1909S, Indian Head Cent, PCGS VF25

Moreover, a very curious way to identify coins is linked to the "verse" of the coin.

Normally all coins have two faces with reverse minting, that is if we turn a coin on its vertical axis (that is, by holding it between two fingers, we rotate it sideways) we will see that, almost always, the figure that appears to us turns out to be upside down. We said "normally" and in fact, the reverse axis, at 180°, is defined as "coin" (or even "French") precisely to distinguish it from the "medal" (or "German") one where instead the two faces are at 0°.

However, there is no precise rule, it depends on the coins: if we examine the South African Krugerrand we see that the two faces have the same direction, if we take the American dollar instead, we realize that the coinage is reversed.

Another step to be able to identify a coin concern wear and tear. It usually occurs as a result of rubbing with other materials or money, which varies according to their nature, deteriorating and wearing out the surface due to prolonged use, resulting in a decrease in the weight of the metal.

All coins, especially the decimal ones, have had daily use due both to operations of ordinary trade and returning in large quantities for transactions with the movement of small and large capitals. In the past, very little circulated, almost exclusively in copper pieces, a little less in silver, and almost nothing in gold. The latter was very rare, difficult to find and the prerogative of the wealthiest castes (just think that during the Kingdom of Sardinia with a 20 Lire gold coin from the period of Carlo Alberto or Carlo Felice or Vittorio Emanuele II, you could buy a cow, a very precious good that was enough to support the nutrition of a large family, natural life during).

Yet these coins, both in gold and in silver, are almost always very worn and in a poor state of conservation: for the coinage of the Kingdom of Sardinia, among the most difficult of the decimal series, the beautiful quality is nowhere to be found. The motivation is simple: the gold coins did not circulate or very little, the silver ones had a current use, and both were used for commercial transactions; there were no institutions that carried out monetary or credit operations, that guarded values or that acted as intermediaries in circulation: they were kept in private coffers or safes.

For payments, once transported, the coin cases were entrusted to experts who checked their weight and authenticity and then the pieces were counted after being struck on a special marble to verify their silvery and golden sound.

This practice was repeated thousands of times, with the consequence of considerably wearing out the coins, to the point of causing a significant drop in weight: on several occasions the state ordered the withdrawal of specimens that were too disfigured or worn out, to replace them with brand new ones. In fact, these not only appeared to be extremely worn, but above all, they were of a weight that no longer corresponded to the original one and was rejected both by the mint and by the market. This passage justifies the rarity of even common coins in Brilliant Uncirculated or Exceptional conservation, while it explains the large quantity of practically smooth pieces present in the numismatic environment: they are the ones rejected because of decreasing weight.

Evaluation criteria

Observing a coin and assigning it a correct degree of conservation is difficult and requires great experience. It is necessary to examine it carefully, look at it several times consider a whole series of possible alterations, evaluate its evident and hidden defects and proceed with the appraisal.

Lines, scratches, minting and falling strokes, repeated strokes, washings, artificial coatings and more all have a decisive influence on the final evaluation of an appraisal.

Stripes and strokes.

The minting strokes are small and follow one another along the entire edge and in the field of the coin. In the coinage of the Sardinian Realm, they are more evident and even more marked, they can be recognized because they are numerous, small and clear-cut, and do not show abrasions from a file, hammer or other. The blows from accidental falls are much more evident and disfiguring, they can be clearly seen when the specimens show traces of restoration, almost always hidden by an artificial patina.

The minting lines are infinitesimal and contrast with the lines from wear or accidental because the former, even if evident, do not damage the quality except, in value, the latter instead always present attempts at restoration, with smoothing produced by small hoses at high speed.

Patines

Coins should be collected in the state in which they are found, as historical and lived objects, but unfortunately, the practice of washing them with special liquids is widespread, which in addition to eliminating their charm also removes their original patina, a small piece of history in the time it took to form. The patinas that can be found in coins of all times are of various types: patinas from the ground, sand, paper, wood, velvet, leather, and more. The false patina, on the other hand, has the particularity of covering defects and differs from an original patina because it is always uniform and without shadows or reflections, with very strong colors.

Jewelry store

it is necessary to pay attention because many coins come from jewelry artifacts, a very common practice in the 19th and 20th centuries. Coins were worn in jewels such as necklaces, pendants, pendants, rings, bracelets or brooches, worn for ostentation or show off. They were soldered or closed in the jewel with staples, and with time and use they have altered in contact with the skin and fabrics. Having been welded with other metals they are disfigured. Then there remain very evident signs of the closing clips when they are removed from the frame and when the hook is removed to eliminate the welding. These imperfections are masterfully eliminated, and the blows are skillfully picked up. For other coins, there was the custom of making a suspension hole and wearing them as pendants or flaunting them in watch chains. These holes are now filled up, but even in this case, traces of the restoration remain.

Portraits

In some cases, the facial features and hair, beard and mustache of the portrait are reconstructed on very worn coins. These remakes take place by means of incisions. The features of the face and bust appear decidedly marked, while the hair, beard and mustache stand out because they are too different from the rest of the coin, generally very worn.

Variants

There are coins cleverly counterfeited to create variations on the master coin or to counterfeit very rare coins. A particular alteration occurs in mint marks, dates or dots. Mint marks are skillfully erased, as are dots, and date numbers are modified or replaced – all done on genuine coins. This custom dates back to the 70s and 80s; the alterers replaced the letters of the mint sign, as in the case of the Turin mint during the Napoleonic occupation: on the reverse, the French mint sign A of Paris was replaced with the letter U, mint of Turin. Also, in the case of the proof coins, or proofs of the Kingdom of Italy, the wording was deleted to allow them to enter normal circulation: these are authentic coins, minted in the mint, but born as proofs. In numismatic collecting, there is a large number of variant coins. It is a series that often hides a pitfall: in fact, all the specimens with small minting parts missing differ from the sample coin, thus constituting a variant. I believe that a coin with an imperfection not caused by the hand of man can be considered a variant such as an off-center minting, overlapping of symbols or letters as happens on the edges of Carlo Felice's coins of Sardinia, or smaller mint marks, or dots in more. On the other hand, when a letter, or a symbol, or a dot or something else is missing, they inevitably arouse a legitimate suspicion of counterfeiting. Some of these variants exist, but since this is an extremely delicate topic, it is advisable to proceed with extreme caution.

Styles

The style of a coin differs from the minting. The first coins minted always had a clear engraving with Mirror Funds and a splendid sparkle. These were the first coins that were brought to rulers to ascertain their beauty and quality: they were presentation or ostentation coins, and they were generally of a beautiful style. Subsequently, with the wear of the coinage, the coin, although Brilliant Uncirculated quality, no longer presented a clear engraving and Mirror Funds, while the glitter disappeared and the style appeared almost amorphous because the worn coinage no longer reflected the strength of the beautiful quality. Then they proceeded to move on to a new mint and restarted the beating, with the same mint but almost always with a different style.

Where to find the value of that coin?

So, once you have identified your coins, now let's see where you can find the value of the coins. When it comes to dealing with places where to find the value of a coin, the first to check is NGC and PCGS price guides. These are the right numismatic guides where you can find all prices of each coin. But if there is something you must know is that normally NGC and PCGS prices are higher than market prices

Another way to have some coin value is to check sites and online auctions to sell and exchange coins.

eBay is one of the sites that can really help you understand the price trend and you can also find the value of the coin you have. But, as anyone can list a price on eBay, only sold auction prices have any real significance.

You can proceed this way:

✓ Go to eBay and use the search bar to look for your coin. To facilitate the process, utilize the identifying format you already know.

✓ Identify the buying format and change it to "Auction".

✓ Find the Filters (normally on the right side of the web page) and go to More Filters.

✓ Go to the Show only Tab and Sold Items. This will display the list of all coins that were sold in an auction taking your search as a reference.

✓ Compare your coin with the listed coins and write down the prices of the most similar ones. This way you will have a range of prices from which to start.

If you are an absolute beginner this range could help you get an idea of the value, but it will be more difficult to verify the state of conservation of your coin to find a more accurate price. So, how do you establish the state of conservation instead in order to be able to evaluate it? You have to patiently check the coin by looking at it with a magnifying glass and weighing it on a scale, but only experts are able to offer a correct evaluation. Some online auctions have teams of professionals who can do it for you.

It is not easy to define the state of conservation of a coin: giving a classification through specific gradual subdivisions is perhaps the most complex of the operations that are usually performed in numismatics, both for the scientific rigor that must be applied, and because being able to bring back a work coined in several copies to an aesthetic category that does not pass through exclusively personal but universally shared criteria is not an easy undertaking.

The beauty of a coin specimen lies in the correct proportion of all intrinsic elements: style, patina, and quality of the engravings. Even in the presence of abrasions, blows, wear due to traffic and the like, it is necessary to evaluate the coordination and harmonious distribution of the whole.

Having said that, never think of going to the bank to have your coins appraised, because the value varies according to the interest shown by collectors, and they are the right interlocutors to turn to. Exactly as happens with antiques. The ideal is therefore to contact a numismatic shop (or Local Coin Shop), they are equipped with the instruments needed to examine a coin's metal content and should be knowledgeable enough to correctly identify and value coins, but once you know the value, we recommend you evaluate other options before selling.

Could be helpful to talk directly with other collectors, being more convenient due to the absence of commission for the shopkeeper-intermediary. But it is even riskier due to possible scams unless you know the collector, he hasn't been recommended to you by someone you trust, or you don't rely on certified online sites that allow you to evaluate its credibility through specific feedback.

Some final tip

Here are some final tips before you take your coin in for grading. It is absolutely not necessary to clean or subject your coins to any kind of treatment to make them shinier and shinier. These operations could greatly compromise the value of the coins to the point of almost nullifying their collecting interest and resale.

Also, remember that live viewing is required for coin valuation.

In order to carry out a correct coin valuation, two fundamental characteristics must be established:

✓ Rarity

✓ Degree of conservation

When carrying out an appraisal, acronyms such as those indicated in the previous chapter are used by convention to indicate these characteristics.

With these tips, we conclude our chapter. In the penultimate part of the guide, we will deal specifically with how to sell your coin collection.

CHAPTER 4: WHAT SHOULD I DO WITH MY INHERITED COIN COLLECTION?

It is not something that happens every day, but if you have rare coins in your hands and that have a particularly high value (such as some 2-euro coins from the Vatican City), and you have managed to create a collection, you will surely be wondering where to take it and how to sell or exchange it. The right answer is not the Bank, as we told you in the previous chapter, because the valuation of a rare coin is given by the interest of numismatic collectors, so it is necessary to get in touch with these subjects. It could then be the case to contact numismatic shops or private collectors directly: the former must pay a commission for the dealer-intermediary, not for the latter, because the sale is direct.

But even in this case, you need to be careful because of possible scams: if you contact a private person, you should either know him previously or that he is a trusted person, suggested by friends and acquaintances. We will talk specifically about counterfeits in the next chapter. Below we will see how and where to sell your coin collection.

How to sell a coin collection?

So now let's see how to sell your coin collection.

Now that you're sure that your coins have a certain value, and you've had them valued correctly, you may be wondering how to sell your collection. We tell you right away that there are very valid sites online for selling and/or exchanging rare coins, for example through auctions that allow you to sell them for free, in some cases offering an expert evaluation.

In this case, there is also the guarantee of the intermediary and the possibility of tracing the coins by following their transit and establishing a reserve price below which the buyer cannot go down. Not to mention the possibility of evaluating the reviews of the sellers, in case of purchase, which allows you to understand who is trusted and who is not.

Some auctions also have notification systems that notify you when the specimen of your interest is being auctioned by others. The further advantage of selling coins on online sites is also that of being able to follow every single phase without physically going to any shop. For example, many sites make numismatic experts available to evaluate your rare pieces at no cost.

But which are the most used sites? First of all, we remember eBay, where you can find specimens of every type and price, then the Catawiki auctions, widely used by numismatists and collectors, on which you can register for free by taking advantage of advice from experts. But it will be in the next paragraph that we will better explain where you can sell your coin collection.

Where to sell your coin collection?

The best solution to sell your coin collection is certainly to turn to sites to exchange and sell rare coins, some online auctions allow you to sell them without paying anything and with the possibility of obtaining an evaluation by an expert.

In this case, there is also the possibility of establishing a minimum price beyond which those who want to buy cannot go down.

The most used sites to see rare coins are the following.

Catawiki

The first professional site to sell rare coins, or eventually buy them, is Catawiki this is an auction site very popular with numismatic collectors, you can register for free and get advice from experts. It is the latest generation site, which you can manage completely online, both via desktop web mode (i.e., from your browser) and via app for mobile devices.

In a few minutes, you can open an account by entering your data and a valid e-mail address. Once the account has been confirmed, you can immediately put your coins on sale, or any other collectible or used item.

One of the most interesting advantages of Catawiki is the presence of different experts, divided by category, able to estimate and value the coin in your possession. If you have no idea what price to put, the expert will immediately indicate a starting value.

Catawiki allows you to auction coins, including a reserve price for those with a higher value. The highest bidder wins the good. As for commissions, we find 9% paid by the buyer and 12.5% paid by the seller.

eBay

eBay, is one of the most famous online marketplaces for second-hand goods, but also for new goods in the world. It is one of the best-known sites ever and there are many collectors who offer specimens of all kinds for sale. By accessing the official page, you can proceed with a quick registration, which allows you to create an account in seconds.

Once this is done, you can insert your coins, taking care to upload more photos (from different angles), choose the right sales category and write an accurate description, which can attract the attention of collectors and numismatics enthusiasts.

eBay allows you to choose different ways of selling. The first is direct sales, i.e., by setting a single purchase price. The second is instead the sale by auction, with a functioning very similar to that of Catawiki, where the highest bidder wins the good.

When the coin is sold, eBay charges a final value fee. The fee is calculated as a percentage of the total sale, plus a fixed value of €0.35 per transaction. The commission is 5% for sales up to €2,000 and 2% over €2,000.

Collectors Universe Forums:

These are forums in which, in addition to having a lot of information on coins, including value and prices, you can find ideal buyers for selling your collection of coins.

Reddit : r/coins4sell and r/coinsales

Just as eBay is another site where you can find buyers willing to buy your coin collecting.

Nomisma

A final solution to sell rare coins is Nomisma. It has been a concrete point of reference for years now for enthusiasts of specific auctions in the numismatics sector. By registering quickly, you can access many exclusive services.

To obtain an estimate and evaluation of your assets, you can contact the company directly, which will analyze the coins, as well as any documents in your possession on the authenticity and possible traceability of the rare piece. Once the coins are entered in lots, with their base price, they can subsequently be sold on the market. Collectors can place their bids and follow the status of the auction even live. To sum up, Nomisma allows you to buy and sell and consult past and still active auctions. However, it is essential to establish the state of conservation of the coin, to understand how to evaluate the piece.

Contact a collector

If you want to sell your rare coins to a collector, there are many legal solutions you can use. Many of the platforms that we have indicated above allow you to speak directly with the interested collector.

For example, you can start a chat, ask for an email and enter into direct negotiation. In this way, you can subsequently offer him other sales, if you own more than one rare, ancient or limited-edition coin. Another solution to be able to contact coin collectors is to use the now well-known social channels, such as Instagram or Facebook. On the same, there are many public groups, with thousands of collectors who can be contacted privately.

Finally, let's remember the forums on numismatics. Inside you can find lots of information on the procedures for selling coins, which auctions or sites to use, and also have the opportunity to talk to many expert collectors ready to buy coins.

After the discussion on how to sell your coin collection in a legal and safe way, in the last chapter we will talk about counterfeit coins and how to recognize them.

CHAPTER 5: SPOTTING A COUNTERFEIT COIN

In this last chapter, we briefly see the history of counterfeiting and how to distinguish a real coin from a fake one.

History of counterfeited coins

In this paragraph, we would like to retrace some historical stages of coin counterfeiting.

According to statistics, the 20-euro banknote and the two-euro coin are the most counterfeited by counterfeiters. Despite the speed of reproduction, each of us runs the risk of finding a counterfeit ticket in our hands sooner or later. Counterfeiting has very ancient origins: its history starts from the ancient sestertii of the Roman Empire, passing through the gold coins of the Middle Ages and the florins of Florence and the Duchies of Venice, and reaches up to today.

Often the fakes have represented real works of art, artistically "more beautiful than the originals". The course of history is dotted with attempts to combat the counterfeiting of money, such as the emperor Augustus, who between 23 and 20 BC attempted, with limited success, to combat the spread of counterfeiting.

The reform desired by the emperor Augustus between 23 and 20 a.C had the precise objective of restoring the solder to precise technical characteristics and compliance with the exchange ratio. Precisely in an attempt to counter the spread of counterfeiters. In the three hundred years that separate the reigns of Augustus and Constantine, the solidus also lost more than 40 percent of its weight while maintaining the purity of the fineness. But the imitators always complied, coating the lead with a patina of gold.

However, the rules of Augustus managed to contain the spread of fakes. In fact, even the Goths decided to leave the technical characteristics of gold coinage unchanged, not only in terms of weight but also in the types of obverse and reverse, which respectively reproduced the busts of the Eastern emperor and of Victory with a jeweled cross. In fact, it was not permitted for any barbarian ruler to imprint his own image on a starter. And even the Arab dinar had the same weight as the imperial and Byzantine solidus.

A novelty was the introduction of the banknote: The first to introduce the use of paper banknotes was the Chinese Emperor Hien Tsung in 806 AD. Those who owned precious metal had an interest in depositing it with operators specialized in its conservation and protection from thieves. Furthermore, he had an interest in turning to bankers to transfer the precious metals without having to undertake expensive and risky transport. It was enough to transfer the document and collect the metal from a second goldsmith-banker, connected to the first by business ties. But not even this introduction defeated the phenomenon of counterfeiting, and counterfeiters simply switched from counterfeiting coins to counterfeiting banknotes.

Modern euro banknotes descended from the first banknotes, which were no exception in terms of counterfeiting, despite the declarations of European technicians who maintained that these new banknotes were impossible to counterfeit.

The first Carolingian king, Pepin the Short, kept the Roman libra in use, his son Charlemagne replaced it with a new one of 410 grams. And the origins of the credit system date back to the Middle Ages. When the need arises to identify valid alternatives to the physical transport of money and valuables. This is how payment through "letters of credit" spread. But the birth of the first credit card will come much, much later. In 1950. It was the Diners club that introduced it, it was intended only for businessmen and used in tourist and entertainment services.

The exhibition also presents some "false state", of "compulsory imitation" for commercial reasons. One of the most recent cases concerns Italy during the colonial adventure in Africa. The fascist authorities had to take note that unlike what happened in Libya and Somalia, our lire were not accepted by the Eritrean populations accustomed to the silver thalers of Maria Theresa of Austria. So, in 1918 it was decided to mint a coin that had the same characteristics. A perfect copy, but one that underlined the Italian authority. Between 1935 and 1939, 19,446,729 "true" Austrian thalers were minted in Rome.

One of the real practical examples to make this journey through time and understand the counterfeiting of coins, with rare pieces and some specimens from the royal collection of Vittorio Emanuele III in Italy, the most important in the world of medieval Italian coins, kept in the vault of the National Museum of Palazzo Massimo. Alongside the original pieces, copies. To show how forgery techniques have followed one another and developed over the centuries.

Some banknotes are artistically more beautiful than the originals". And if the lie of the modern currency is usually in the design, in the ancient and medieval world the distinction between true and false is linked to the goodness of the metal used and to the weight of the coin.

How to identify fake?

In this last paragraph, we will explain step by step and differentiate details for gold coins, and silver coins. Nowadays, there are many ancient coins on the market. And if by chance, one has fallen into your hands or you have inherited it from some family collection, it is good that you verify its veracity by following a few small precautions. It may surprise you, yet there are many forgers who work on the reproduction of coins of all ages and origins. Precisely for this reason, we have decided to provide you with a small guide that can help you recognize the authenticity and value of ancient coins. To verify its quality and value, it is important to follow and respect small precautions. Contrary to what one might think, in fact, there are many counterfeiters present in this sector.

This world, in fact, is very rich and presents coins of every age and origin and is mainly divided between those in silver and those in gold.

Silver and other coins

Before providing you with useful information for recognizing your coins, it should be noted that only those minted before the 18th century are considered ancient when the mints used materials such as silver, gold, bronze, copper and orichalcum. So, antique silver coins are only considered antique if they were minted before the 18th century. Having clarified this, remember to always have a magnifying glass with you to inspect the coin in detail. As far as silver coins are concerned, for example, it is advisable to carefully check the patination that is created on the surface: in most cases, silver tends to darken over time, almost to the point of obtaining a blackish color. But even this patina can be reproduced by counterfeiters, so it is good that you observe the coin in all its details. Then check that there are small creases along the edges, due to the hammer blows that were given on the minting during the minting procedure. Finally, true experts will be able to recognize a real silver coin by the sound it produces when touching other coins.

This classification is due to the fact that later the State Mints began to use materials, in addition to silver, also in gold, bronze, copper and orichalcum.

To evaluate the value, it is important to be equipped with a magnifying glass capable of inspecting the coin in detail. In the case of silver objects, it is important to examine the patination present on the surface: this metal in fact tends to darken over time. For experts in the sector, on the other hand, it will be easy to recognize whether it is a valuable object based on the sound it produces when it touches other coins.

Gold antiques

The most beautiful and precious ancient coins are certainly those in gold. In fact, more valuable than silver coins are gold coins. But they are also the most difficult to recognize, especially taking into account the fact that gold does not produce any kind of patina and that gold coins were often melted down to use the precious metal for another minting. However, these are very difficult to recognize both because they do not have the patina and because in the past, they were melted down to use this precious metal in other coinages as well.

Beyond this, using the magnifying glass with great skill, you will have the possibility to recognize whether your coin is real or not. Check well for any errors in writing or drawings, and check if the plating is hasty, which is often recurrent in fakes.

The only factor that can help in establishing whether it is a real coin or not is to check if there are any errors in writing or drawings on it. An inaccuracy often present in counterfeits is that of having inserted a hasty plating: checking this factor allows you to establish whether you are dealing with an authentic or a fake coin.

BOOK 3: FROM ZERO TO HERO

Introduction

Here we are at the third guide for you who want to become a coin collector and don't know where to start. In fact, in this book, you will find all the steps necessary to make a collection of coins with all the credentials in order.

This guide will be divided into 11 chapters all relating to the steps and precise rules to have your splendid and profitable collection of coins.

We are sure that, after having understood how the anatomy and the coin market work, thanks to this third guide you will finally be able to realize your numismatic wishes.

And you can do it completely from scratch, setting your intentions and goals and looking for the most beautiful and rarest coins in the world.

CHAPTER 1: WHERE DO I START?

Well, we are here to quickly explain and introduce to you, in this first chapter, how to start, completely from scratch, to create your personal coin collection.

How to start from zero?

As we already know, one usually starts collecting coins as a hobby.

Many believe that you have to buy coins to start a collection, but you can start with just the change you have in your pocket. Others may start a collection out of historical rather than artistic interests. Some people collect coins for investment purposes only, such as gold or silver coins.

A really important thing to do, therefore, when starting from scratch, is precisely to set goals and define a correct strategy.

Whatever the reason that prompted you to start collecting rare coins, you are in the right place. Read our next advice and our step-by-step strategy for the next chapters and follow your way in this fantastic world. Anyway, going back to the step-by-step strategy for building your own coin collection from scratch, it will consist of the following steps. Steps that will be deepened, one by one, in the next chapters. So, you will have to:

1. Identify your motivation.
2. Choose the theme of your collection.
3. Go deeper and include a database check for making a coin desired list inside the chosen category and where to fins cheat sheets to be quicker.
4. Set a budget.
5. Start your coin hunting.
6. Handling, cleaning and storing your collection.
7. Catalog your collection.
8. Selling your collection.

Here these will be the main steps to work on in order to have a winning strategy that will allow you to create a real coin business.

CHAPTER 2: IDENTIFY YOUR MOTIVATION

In this second chapter, we will deal with the first fundamental step for your coin collection or the setting of objectives. Why do you want to collect coins? What is the motivation that drives you to do it? These are the first questions you need to ask yourself.

What could be the reason for starting your own coin collection?

First absolute step to start collecting valuable coins: ask yourself why you want to do it. There are several reasons, in fact, that could have prompted you to create your own coin collection and we will specifically indicate the main ones below. Choose yours and start setting your goals.

Business

Let's start with one of the most popular motivations, which is to create a business. Why not make money with coins? The business is one of the reasons that is linked to the main objective of profiting from a possible exchange or sale of coins. Tell the truth, that's not what you thought about. If the answer is yes, you will probably have to commit yourself even more to looking for the rarest and most beautiful coins with an optimal state of conservation, to say the least.

Hobby

Another of the main reasons people start looking for and collecting coins is for fun. In fact, collecting coins is considered a useful hobby, which could help to distract us from the stresses and problems of everyday life. Not to mention the fact that you can get us away from hobbies, which more than hobbies could represent real vices.

Familiar idea

Another reason to collect coins could be to involve your family members (especially children) in a totally educational activity to do together. You could do it to teach your children to recognize certain countries or historical periods, but also how to take care of objects and get passionate about something useful.

Historic interest

Perhaps you are passionate about a certain period of history or perhaps a particular country. Maybe you like some distinctive designs or engravings or maybe you are a fan of rare metals like gold or silver. There are so many possibilities but whatever your path, you have to understand what you like and what fascinates you. In this way you will be able to better manage your budget, investing only in the pieces that really interest you.

Curiosity

There are those who might decide to start collecting coins, simply out of curiosity, to enrich their knowledge and culture. Knowing the world through the objects that have made its history is an exciting and extraordinary experience for many, so starting a coin collection could be something really positive.

These are the main reasons, so just choose the one closest to you. Having done this, in the next chapter, we will present you with another important choice, namely the theme of your coin collection.

CHAPTER 3: CHOOSE THE COLLECTING CATEGORY THAT BEST FIXES YOU

Well, have you chosen your motivation and set goals? Once this is done, the time has come to choose the category of coins you want to collect and, in this chapter, we will address this issue.

Choosing your coin collection category

Here is a mini guide that will help you choose the theme or category of your coin collection, based on your tastes and needs. Let's see what the main categories are. As well as the reasons, evaluate a bit which one best fixes you.

Theme

When we talk about the topic, we are talking in general about all those listed below. Theme can be historical, geographical, cultural, or simply by the material used. In fact, you could decide to go in search of only silver or gold coins. The choice of theme, however, remember that it always depends on your goals. But choosing a theme could relate to much more, such as a fictional or historical character, a scientist, animals, cars, railways, flowers, sports, celebrities or sporting events. Know that one of the most popular themes chosen for the coin collection is the Olympic Games, closely followed by football and military history.

Historical significance

If you are a history buff, coins can be an ideal link to that particular historical period of your interest. Are you determined to collect coins from Ancient Rome, or Ancient Greece? Well, you choose the historical significance that suits you best.

Denomination

The easiest way to start a coin collection is with the denomination in mind, i.e., you may decide to create a euro coin collection. Or a collection of dollars. They are nice coins representative of the states you are interested in and quite easy to find.

The most common specimens can be found directly in the rest of the shopping. It is always exciting to check the loose change and find just the coin we needed to complete the collection of a particular euro country. Other coins, including rare euro or dollar coins, can be found at affordable numismatic auctions and can be procured without much effort.

Country of origin

The currency has acquired prestige, and in some cases has also had the role of advertising medium, especially in times when the means of communication were slow and dangerous, and most people were illiterate. Coins bear witness to important events, such as the construction of monuments or the re-enactment of battles. So if you are interested in a particular country, its conquests, battles, victories or defeats, collecting coins of that particular country can help you reconstruct its history and vicissitudes.

Cherry picking

Making a comparison with cherry picking, from a psychological point of view, collecting means preserving objects that for us have value, and meaning and that lead to aesthetic and sensory pleasure, capable of representing an excellent anxiolytic, just like a doll is in the arms of a child. To collect is to put it in order. And whoever is a collector knows this very well. Moments of absolute relaxation are spent reviewing one's collection, dusting it, cleaning it and putting it back in its place. In fact, you could choose coins in chronological order and the rarest to find and create a collection on this very theme.

Another creative way

There are other more creative motivations that drive us to create somewhat unusual coin collections. For example, there are those who could decide to collect all the coins minted in their own year of birth or that of their children.

This concludes our second step of the strategy to start a coin collection from scratch. Let's see, in the next chapter what the next step will be.

CHAPTER 4: GO DEEPER

The third step to building a coin collection from scratch is an invitation to dig deeper. Below we will explain what we are talking about.

Start to list your desired coin

Once you have set your motivations, and goals and chosen the theme of your collection, you will now be able to understand what kind of coins you are looking for. By doing thorough research, the next step is simply to create one "database check" for making a coin desired list.

You should set all this coin wish list inside the chosen category.

In short, it is simply a matter of going and listing all the coins that you already know you will need to create your dream collection.

In this case, you can create an excel sheet on your computer and tick off the coin every time you find it.

When we find it, it will be important to check it from the wish list and insert it in another database that will concern the coins owned (more on this later in this guide).

For the more romantic or nostalgic ones, a notebook or pen and paper will do just fine.

The important thing is to have a note of the coins we want and to find them one by one.

Also, remember to find a system where to find cheat sheets to be quicker in your research.

The wish list must then entirely concern your motivations and the chosen category.

Here are some ideas on how to name your databases:

✓ You could collect foreign coins or those from your own country.

✓ You could collect coins of small denominations or those of larger denominations.

✓ You may like to collect coins in folders to try to complete the series in circulation in your life.

✓ You may enjoy collecting uncirculated, uncirculated coins such as those available in the United States since the 1950s.

✓ You may enjoy collecting uncirculated, uncirculated coins that were struck for collectors.

✓ You may collect uncirculated silver sets (cheaper than gold ones) that are very beautiful, and their value will increase (or decrease) according to fluctuations in the price of silver.

Here are some ideas on how to do it. Once this database has been created, you will finally be able to move on to a decisive step that will be explained to you in the next chapter, namely establishing a budget to create your coin collection.

CHAPTER 5: SET A BUDGET

Now that you know which theme you have chosen based on your motivations and objectives and created the list of coins that you want to have in your collection, the time has come to establish a price. In this case, we are not talking about the selling price, but about the purchase. In short, we are talking about budgets, and we will explain them better below.

Setting your coin collection budget

We have reached the fourth step: after having cataloged, and established categories and objectives, it is right that a possible coin collection should be feasible in practice. And for this reason, it becomes essential to think about and choose a precise budget for your collection.

Perhaps you are passionate about a certain period of history or perhaps a particular country. Maybe you like some distinctive designs or engravings or maybe you are a fan of rare metals like gold or silver. There are so many possibilities but whatever your path, you have to understand what you like and what fascinates you. In this way you will be able to better manage your budget, investing only in the pieces that really interest you.

This budget will be based entirely on your financial possibilities, above all, on how much you are willing to spend, and on which coins you have placed your attention.

We want to reiterate one important thing about the budget: you don't always have to spend a fortune. Very often, we find ancient and rare coins at home because they were left by parents or grandparents perhaps in some tin can or old piggy bank. Finding some ancient coins in the attic is a way like any other to start collecting them. Not to mention the fact that you can start simply with the change you have in your pocket when you go shopping.

You can also decide to ask friends and family if they have old coins and if they can be had, or offer to buy them, based on what seems appropriate to your budget.

Therefore, to start a coin collection it is good to start from the base, therefore from the easiest coins to find. S The most common specimens are easily found, even among the remains of the shopping. By checking the pennies, in fact, you will be able to see a variety of images and complete the first collection of a particular European country. If some are missing, it will be possible to buy them during numismatic auctions, where prices are affordable, and coins will be procured without any effort.

It is rather obvious to say that the more capital you have available for your budget, the more you will have the possibility to finish your coin collection or simply reinvest to sell them and make a profit. You will say, I want a collection entirely free or the maximum I can spend is 100 dollars, for example. Just remember that before you decide to spend money on coins, learn everything you can about them and especially do the first three steps. You can very well start with loose change in your pocket and familiarize yourself with their parts, inscriptions, images, what material it is made of and what kind of coin it is. Once you learn the basics and follow the first 3 steps, you'll soon be able to evaluate the best approach to budgeting your collection.

Now that you've established your budget, it's time to move on to the real action in the next chapter, which is coin hunting.

CHAPTER 6: START THE COIN HUNTING

In this chapter, we will move on to the firth step of your coin collection strategy and explain where to locate the coins.

How can I "hunt" my coins?

A first way to hunt for coins, and we have already illustrated to you when we talked about budgets, is by checking the coins you will be able to see a variety of images and complete the first collection of a specific geographical country. If some are missing, it will be possible to buy them during numismatic auctions, where prices are affordable, and coins will be procured without any effort and your hunt will be easy.

Another next step is that relating to the rarer dollar. Finding it at home is quite common. Just check the pockets of old coats of parents but also grandparents, in old piggy banks or jars left there for years. After having found them, it is good to clean them up but be careful, only if it is deemed necessary. Otherwise, you can store them in the appropriate transparent boxes for coins or plastic containers (but we will talk deeper about it in the next chapters). The watchword for numismatics is research. Whether you start collecting dollars, euros, pounds, or other older coins from different eras. Quests are for learning everything you can about what you're collecting. This way it will be easy to evaluate. You will learn to distinguish the valid ones from the fake ones, the worn ones that have no value and the hard ones to find. The value is essential to be able to later estimate the collection. The story, on the other hand, is used for personal knowledge about an anecdote that is hidden behind an ancient coin. If you are passionate about a certain historical period or a certain country, you will surely love the coins of that era. Find particular engravings that make your piece unique and that's why you want to own them all. For this intention to become real and enter your collection, it will be necessary to invest a certain budget in purchases but also in conservation which must be careful. Be careful, though, invest only in what you think is worth it. On this topic, it is necessary to say a few words about sellers. Not everyone is honest in the field of numismatics. Therefore, it is advisable to be careful not to fall into the traps set up by some collectors who only want to make money on those who are perhaps less experienced. For this reason, choose to rely on safe buying and selling services, avoiding underestimating your collector's items and above all making sure you are not buying or selling a fake piece.

The figure of an intermediary is important. He will be the one to guarantee the quality and authenticity of the coin, thanks to the control systems but above all to the right experience in the field of numismatics. You can also increase your collection by going to coin exhibitions. You can also visit local retailers to look for bargains, and you can almost always find a cheap coin container suitable for both children and adults.

Acquiring Coins: where?

It is essential, before investing in coins, as we said, that you follow all the previous steps and invest in knowledge of the numismatics hobby. You should have at least one reference book that covers your area of interest.

Whether you've found coins in your house or are collecting circulating coins from various countries you need to do some research. One of the best ways to "buy and sell carefully" is to read up before buying. There are many books on the market and our guides are just for clarifying all your doubts. Then there are books available on specific series (Lincoln Cent), and types (ancient coins, mints, gold coins, tokens and medals, etc.). There are books that are important for establishing the value of coins. Books available commercially or in libraries cover all topics related to coin collecting or numismatics. Knowledge lies in understanding the difference between a rare coin and a common one. This is because you have to learn everything you can about the coins you own. In this way, you will be able to evaluate for yourself which coins are good, which are false, which are too worn and therefore of no value, which are common, and which are rare. To find out how to tell if a coin is counterfeit, we refer you to the fifth chapter of the second guide.

After that, coins can be acquired in several ways:

✓ Asking friends and acquaintances traveling abroad to bring you coins in the normal course of circulation of the countries they visit.

✓ Searching in second-hand markets, or more specifically of a numismatic nature.

✓ Buying coins at auctions.

✓ Numismatic Associations often offer members the opportunity to purchase coins at reasonable prices.

✓ In specialized shops.

✓ Exchanging coins with other collectors.

✓ Searching the Internet.

✓ In Embassies and Consulates.

✓ Check with your local banks or financial institutions. Many sell wallets or bags of coins at face value.

Ended this discussion about coins hunting, let's see, in the next chapter how to handle, clean and store your coin collection.

CHAPTER 7: HANDLING, CLEANING AND STORING YOUR COLLECTION

We continue this third practical guide with the maintenance and cleaning of your coins. Now that you have bought or acquired them, in fact, it is right to preserve your collection in the best possible way, whether you simply want to keep it at home or, even more so, sell it.

How to handle your coin collection

First of all, let's see how best to handle your coins, to ensure that they last over time.

Now that you have collected all of your coins for now, you will need to store them very carefully to protect them from damage and theft. Conservation is essential so that the collection does not lose value in each of its pieces, but above all none of these is lost over time due to carelessness or poor maintenance.

First of all, it is necessary to use gloves for the coins, since you will never have to touch them with your fingers. With gloves, it will be easy to handle them, remember to always hold them between the index finger and the thumb. These should be placed in special plastic sheet containers, or in transparent plastic boxes, so as to always keep them visible at home or in your office.

The box, however, may not even be anonymous. In fact, using customized boxes for coins, which illustrate the main characteristics such as the year and country of origin, will help explain to the viewer the period of reference but also its importance. Remember that even sugared almond boxes can be useful for conservation purposes. If you have some transparent and anonymous plastic ones, your coins can also be housed there, provided that no one touches them apart from you and with due precautions.

Ultimately, long-term storage is essential. Collecting your transparent plastic containers in cardboard boxes serves to ensure that the collection is safe, and protected from thermal and external agents. Furthermore, to ensure proper handling and storage of the coins, we will have to take some precautions: ___

✓ Do not overload our coin albums, because if we do we run the risk of tearing the sheets. Moreover, if the sheets are crowded and overloaded, the coins of the different sheets will hit each other quite violently when the pages are turned.

✓ Care must be taken when handling the album. In some, the coins tend to pop out, when flipped, involving the coins in big risks.

✓ Every time the coins are extracted from the sheets of the album, it is necessary to place a soft cloth on the table and avoid carrying out these operations in rooms with a hard floor. If a precious silver coin falls on a tiled floor, the consequences could be dire.

✓ Coins should be removed and handled using a pair of rubber-tipped tweezers so that, as far as possible, the coin pockets of the album are not deformed, and the coin is not touched with the fingers. If you don't have pliers available, you only need to touch the coins from the edge.

✓ Always avoid touching coins with objects or materials that could scratch them.

Simply put, no precautions are superfluous when handling your collection.

How to clean your coins

After understanding the importance of handling your coins correctly, let's see how they need to be cleaned to preserve them properly and keep their appearance intact. Know that one of the most important and discussed topics in the numismatic field is coin cleaning.

First of all, let's assume that coins should never be cleaned. Cleaning can damage coins and reduce their numismatic value. Cleaning is usually done solely for the purpose of archaeological and historical study. There is a proper way to clean coins and using the wrong method can often reduce their value. Anyway, the best advice about cleaning a coin is that this is not absolutely necessary. If you really do wish to clean your coins, the best thing to do is consult a numismatic expert to make it on your behalf. But remember that you should never use chemicals or abrasive cleaning products on your coins. If you are new to cleaning coins, it is probably best to leave them as they are. A hasty or incorrectly performed cleaning can irreparably damage a rare coin. In fact, remember that by cleaning the reliefs of the designs on the coin even only with an abrasive cloth and an unsuitable soap, you can do damage. In particular, you can wear the edges of the reliefs to the point of affecting the quality degree of the coin and therefore its value.

It may happen that for commercial reasons or for personal interests and tastes we come across the need to have or want to clean our beloved coins, but to do so you need experience, technique and the right tools to do it otherwise you risk considerably reducing or sometimes eliminating the value of the coin itself.

Before cleaning a coin, in addition to the metal to be treated, the type of dirt that affects it must also be evaluated, it can be simple earth, grease, encrustations, oxidations, metal cancer, etc.

The separate discussion has coins with patina, which should never be removed as it is a more pleasant element and which in many cases increases the value and beauty of the coin.

Nonetheless, if we are really sure that the coin will not show any damage, we could proceed with the cleaning. Our method will be based on two products: water and neutral soap:

1. Wash the coin in warm running water, so that any dust and earth are removed.

2. Then, using your fingers, gently apply some liquid soap, to both sides of the coin.

3. Finally, rinse the coin with warm water, and dry it with a soft dry cloth.

It is not advisable to brush it, however soft the brush may be. The coin can be scrubbed sparingly, using a fiberglass brush to loosen the dirt, especially on recently unearthed coins. Coins with patina, whether green or black, should not be touched. At the limit, we can brush them with a horsehair brush, to enhance the natural patina brilliance. If after cleaning we see some stains that are not due to rust, we can rub them with a pencil eraser.

Never clean silver coins with chemical products (liquids, powders or soaked cloths) available on the market. Copper and bronze coins can be cleaned using olive oil, letting them dry until they shine. Finally, a golden rule: if after cleaning the coin still seems dirty, leave it alone and don't touch it again! You might only make the situation worse.

How to store your coin collection

We come to the last part of this seventh chapter or how to store your collectible coins.

There are some simple tips we can give you that will help you protect and preserve your precious coins from damage. You don't want to waste the time it took to get a rare coin, after studying, researching and of course investing money, only to have it fall or get damaged because you're holding it the wrong way, right?

In short, keeping coins in perfect condition and organizing them well is an obligation for a numismatist.

As far as storage specifically is concerned, coins made of metal can get damaged really easily, so it's important to handle and store them with care. Indeed, in many ancient coins, there is metal inside of them, and with the exception of gold, and we should say that they can be damaged because of a variety of environmental factors. Bumps and scratches can be caused by contact with other coins, ore by some dust particles, humidity, or cold. But even the oxygen in the air could cause damage and reduce their exchange value. Anyway, with the purchase of some inexpensive items and the adoption of some routine procedures, it can be possible to preserve them in excellent condition for a long time.

Know that the easiest way to keep them is to put them in a purse or in a locker.

Should you start acquiring more valuable and expensive coins, they will require a better storage solution. a good idea is to buy a "certified" coin, i.e., a coin that has been rated by an independent service such as PCGS or NGC. This gives the coin a more concrete value.

The coin purses also represent an ideal solution for storing coins individually. There are also special hermetic envelopes or albums that can be used to store or display a collection of coins, avoiding their oxidation or scratches.

Here are some tips for the passive conservation of our collection:

✓ Do not expose the collection to substances or conditions that could deteriorate, oxidize, deform, etc.

✓ Always keep the collection in environments with stable temperature and humidity conditions.

✓ Gold coins don't need much care. Silver, bronze, copper or iron coins, on the other hand, are very sensitive to corrosion and humidity.

✓ Do not clean coins, especially with products that make them shine.

✓ Don't assume that all old coins are in very bad shape. If you buy coins, on the other hand, don't assume they are in good condition, especially if they are over 500 years old. Of course, as the age of the coin increases, the very good condition adds more value.

✓ Get something to hold the coins. This doesn't mean you have to buy eye-catching purses (although these may keep them in better condition). Coin purses can be quite cheap, or you can use an old shoe box or butter container.

✓ Keep coins in a safe place. If you buy expensive coins, invest in a safe box and containers that won't damage their numismatic value.

Now, it's time to underline an important aspect: the place to store. It will be really important to consider some basic rules, like: "if the environment will be quite comfortable enough for a person, it will probably be comfortable enough for the collection too". If you choose an environment like a cellar (cold and humid) or in the apartment (warm and dry) must be strictly forbidden, to ensure that your coin collection will not deteriorate but, on the contrary, remains in the best possible condition in the time. A bedroom or closet can be the best place to choose.

Now, let's consider another chance to store them: place your precious coins in a safety deposit box. If you want to have one of the safest places to store coins, without a doubt, you must opt for a safety deposit box at your bank. But, this also can be the most expensive solution. A less expensive option is to purchase a personal safe or opt for a briefcase. Then, you can buy some plastic bags or a cardboard porthole in any numismatic shop to keep them safe from exposure to all the elements that could be harmful to your precious coin collection. For the more valuable coins, the most important thing to do is to buy and use hard plastic capsules which offer solid protection.

So, at this point, you should never forget:

✓ To have a silica gel pack. This is in order to absorb excess moisture inside the briefcase or be safe.

✓ Only handle coins when absolutely necessary.

These tips conclude our chapter on handling, cleaning and storing your coins. In the next chapter, however, we will explain how to catalog them.

CHAPTER 8: CATALOG YOUR COLLECTION

In these eight chapters, we will explain how to make an inventory and what information to include to store and collect your coins

How to make an inventory?

First of all, we tell you that cataloging your coin collection is really important because, in addition to being custodians of these miniature works of art, it is necessary to preserve them for future generations, simply to sell them. Now when a coin collection is properly cataloged it will be much easier for your heirs to liquidate your coin collection if they don't want to keep it for themselves. Alternatively, you can use your coin collection catalog to allocate coins to heirs to your estate or as sold. In order to catalog your coins, it is right that you create an inventory where you can classify your coins according to type, date, historical period, etc.

Also in this case, you could create a database directly on your computer or create registers in which to insert the coins that you will be acquiring/purchasing.

When you create your catalog, you should enter the details of exactly what is contained in your collection, how much you paid for it and how much it should be worth on the cataloging date.

There is also special software to catalog your collectibles. In fact, coin cataloging software allows you to catalog in a simple and intuitive way.

It is not the usual program that requires thousands of pieces of information to manage coin cataloging: you will decide how to organize your electronic catalog.

You will be able to define what to display, organize the photos of your coins and thus better manage the cataloging of coins. With an innovative search engine, you can quickly find a valuable piece in your electronic catalog.

One last method that we share is aimed at classifying and maintaining your collection via the app.

This method concerns the use of smartphone applications designed for holding and collecting coins, thus creating a collection and always keeping it under control.

The two main applications for this purpose are the following:

- Maktun.
- Euro coins.

Then there are other applications dedicated exclusively to coin recognition. The two main applications are:

- Coinscope.
- Coin detects.

What information to include?

Until now we have understood that, for the correct classification, and consequent evaluation, it is essential to obtain a good catalog of coins, which covers the area of our interest, in order to be able to search for our coins among its pages.

The most important function of classification is to be able to find as much information about our currency.

For this, the following information must be included and reported in your catalog. This requires you to:

✓ Search in the catalog, for the country that the coin shows if it is foreign and the name of the country is easily legible.

✓ Placing the coin within a particular kingdom or historical period, noting the effigy, the legend or other characteristics.

✓ Insert date of mint, country of origin and so on.

✓ Try to ascertain, through the Mint symbol or the acronym, which Mint minted the coin, in the event that several Mints minted the same coin at the same time.

✓ Be guided by coins having the same face value as ours, or, if this does not exist, by coins of the same material and size.

✓ Note the price value of the cataloging date.

✓ Find the coin in the catalog, compare it with the photographs, and applying the criteria seen before, look for the coin which, by date, legend and type, corresponds exactly to our piece.

Now that you know how to catalog and store your coins, the time has come to take a decisive step that we will explain to you in the next chapter, namely selling your coin collection.

CHAPTER 9: SELLING YOUR COIN COLLECTION

One of the fundamental steps concerning the collection of coins is precisely that of the sale. Obviously, if you simply want a collection to keep and reserve for your heirs, or simply do it as a hobby, you can very well skip this step.

Preliminary information before selling your coin collection

One of the first things to do before thinking about selling your coins is to verify their authenticity. We have already dealt with the discussion in the second guide, here we will delve into some aspects for a moment.

First, some practice or sensitivity is required, which is acquired only after having observed and touched hundreds of coins.

So, it is good practice to establish what type of coins it is: however, dated they may be, they could have little (or even zero) value if there are many of them in circulation. It is certainly necessary to read what the coins bear written, starting from the state or kingdom to which they belong. To be more on the safe side, contact a numismatic expert. After having carried out an accurate search on the internet, you could obtain all the necessary information you need. The state of conservation also affects the value.

However, it is always recommended, if in doubt, to seek advice from an expert who can help us, and from whom we can learn a lot. After that, a very in-depth technical study will allow us to ascertain which group our currency belongs to, whether it is authentic, false or counterfeit. We distinguish the last two cases below:

1. False coin: this coin was created with the intention of defrauding the State, and was designed to be placed in common circulation, together with other legal tender currencies. There is a particular type of counterfeit coin, called a "vintage counterfeit", which can be made of the same metal or even of higher value than the original, and which normally acquires a higher value on the market than the original itself. But of course, most of the fake coins are made of lower-value metal.

2. Counterfeit coin: This coin is conceived with evident criminal intentions, and is made to be used in the numismatic field and in general for coin collecting. It is placed on the market as genuine currency, and the extreme care and perfection it achieves are sometimes unimaginable. In general, counterfeit coins have no value unless they are made of precious metal.

There are some specialized counterfeit coin catalogs on the market. There are also some publications containing sections devoted to counterfeits identified on the market. But if we don't have sufficient experience on the subject, the best thing is undoubtedly to compare the coin in question with one that we know is certainly authentic. We must take a look at details like the sound of the metal, the purity of the coin, the weight, minimal differences in thickness and reliefs, different initials or inscriptions, almost imperceptible differences in the engraving of the shield, hair, shape of the letters, etc.

An important aspect is given precisely by the origin of the coin. It is therefore possible to buy and subsequently sell only coins that circulate with adequate documentation regarding origin and traceability, using the sites presented in the guide.

Choose the perfect moment to sell

Before understanding, which is the right time to sell coins, you must necessarily evaluate the pieces in your possession. They can be sold in numismatic shops, or conveniently online, using professional sites and auctions, such as Catawiki. As already mentioned in the previous guide, after having made a careful evaluation and you are sure that you can make a lot of money from the sale of your collection, you can sell rare coins simply by registering on an online site, such as Catawiki, have the coins from an expert and sell them directly, or auction them.

However, it should be noted that investments in currencies, as assets, are not subject to taxation, with the exception of the surplus value realized at the time of purchase.

But, despite this, there are two ideals time in which you can sell your coin collection.

✓ Around the Florida United Numismatics (FUN) show in January and,

✓ Around the summer American Numismatics Association (ANA) in July or August.

People are in the mood to buy coins, so you are more likely to succeed. This is accurate whether you decide to sell coins privately, on consignment, or at an auction.

Otherwise, if you want to sell billions (of precious metal coins), you should monitor market prices of the specific metal (gold, silver, palladium, platinum) to spot the perfect moment to sell. Since these are commodities, their market value is always liable to change.

If we talk about rare coins, in principle, if the state of conservation is protected, they do not lose value over time. This means that you don't necessarily have to be in a hurry.

As regards, specifically, the right time to sell, know that there is no rigid and valid timing for everyone. The needs are personal: if someone urgently needs liquidity he will tend to push for the sale, even if it is not the most suitable historical moment for the numismatics market. It is a bit like the parallelism we can make for real estate: the ideal, before putting a house up for sale, would be to check the price per square meter. We should also say that personal reasons and urgency could push the sale even in other less profitable moments.

CHAPTER 10: COIN COLLECTOR'S TOOLBOX

Here we are in the tenth chapter, where we will talk about the toolbox. By toolbox, we mean tools for proper handling and preserve, software, official web pages, a webpage to identify and find the value of the coin, and a app mobile for coin collectors. Let's see specifically what it is.

Tools for proper coin handling and preserving

Let's see the right tools for coin handling and preserving that you should have.

For the correct handling and viewing of the pieces, we suggest the following objects and equipment:

✓ A felt cloth or other soft cloth, on which to place the coins during handling.

✓ An album or container in which to store and protect the coins.

✓ A pair of tweezers with rubber or adhesive tape - preferably of the cloth type - on the tips, useful for extracting the coins from the album.

✓ Two magnifying glasses: one very large, with about 10 magnifications, to observe the whole coin; and the other with about 15-20x magnification, to examine the details.

✓ Small paper or plastic bags, to carry coins, or to keep double coins.

✓ A notebook or notebook where you can note the purchase price of each coin, with whom and when the coins were exchanged, or if they were given to you, their state of conservation, their rarity factor, etc.

✓ A good white light, which does not distort colors.

✓ A cabinet or drawer in which to keep the envelopes or albums.

✓ A pair of gloves to handle your coins.

✓ A pair of tweezers with rubber tips, so that, as far as possible, the coin pockets of the album are not deformed, and the coin is not touched with the fingers. If you don't have pliers available, you only need to touch the coins from the edge.

Tools for cataloging and valuing your coins

A valid method to use to know the value and classify the coins in your collection is the book reference. In other words, are books suitable for purchase and use of a numismatic volume/catalog?

There are several numismatic catalogs dedicated to lira coins, and more. It is a sort of coin reference book. As you can see checking on the web there are numerous options to get you started. One of these could be The Official Red Book of United States coins which comes out with a new, updated volume every single year.

If you are going to collect a specific series or focus on coins from another country, you will also find a reference book out there that can give you the details for which coins you are looking.

The catalogs just mentioned containing all the collectible coins with the values of these coins and their state of rarity. By doing so, you can obtain all the information necessary for cataloging and how to classify the coins in your collection.

In order to sell and evaluate our coins, we report the aforementioned apps:

✓ Maktun.

✓ Euro coins.

What about other applications dedicated exclusively to coin recognition. The two main applications are:

✓ Coinscope.

✓ Coin detects.

Consulting up-to-date software could also be a really important tool when it comes to valuing, recognizing and possibly selling your coin collection. Among the best Coin Collecting Software of this year, we have.

✓ **Best Overall:** PCGS Set Registry

✓ **Best for Valuing a Coin Collection:** EzCoin

✓ **Best for U.S. Coins:** US Coin

✓ **Best Coin Collection Inventory Tracker:** Coin Manage

✓ **Best for World Coins:** Exact Change

For what about official web sites we have:

✓ https://www.govmint.com/coin-authority/post/the-best-coin-resources-for-collectors-online

✓ https://www.usmint.gov/

✓ www.royalmint.com

Consulate software, whether they are also the official web page, is a practical and reliable application intended for coin lovers, numismatists or amateurs looking to create a numismatic collection.

With these sites, you will be able to organize and manage your coin collection: create an advanced catalog of your coins, sell and search lists, and view statistics of your collection.

Most of this software offers the following services:

✓ Characteristics.

✓ Nation of money.

✓ Issue details.

✓ Auction information on buying and selling.

✓ Prices and catalog numbers.

✓ Address and point on the map.

After we have finished explaining the best tools for your coin collection, in the final part of this third guide we will take care of giving you all the do's and don'ts that pertain to your coin collection and the rules for its success.

CHAPTER 11: RULES OF SUCCESS IN COIN COLLECTING

We have reached the final chapter of this guide, where we will show you all the rules and tips for a successful coin collection.

Tips and rulers for your successful coin collection

To round off this guide that made you start from scratch up to a collection of coins of a certain importance, here are some rules and useful tips to ensure that this collection really gives you satisfaction. So, the best tips and rules are:

✓ To launch is really important to know what you want to collect. Do some research. Don't hesitate to purchase books that address the theme of your collection. The more books you have on the subject, the more you know about it and the more unbeatable you will be.

✓ The most important tool is patience, but you also need to have many books on the subject. It takes time to build a good collection.

✓ Try to find a theme to collect, to avoid buying everything. Prefer quality over quantity. It is better to buy one coin for 50 euros than 50 coins for 1 euro. You will understand later. Do not hesitate to ask professionals for advice. Join a numismatic club to be able to share your passion. The most important thing in a coin collection is its preservation. Never clean coins. A coin is not worth more because it is very shiny!!!

✓ Try to have a homogeneous collection in terms of quality.

✓ Always keep coins by the edges. This will prevent wear and tear and fingerprints on faces, which are the ones that really matter.

✓ If you intend to buy an expensive coin, a good idea is to buy a "certified" coin, i.e., a coin rated by an independent service such as PCGS or NGC. This gives the coin a more concrete value.

✓ Don't collect cheap coins and treat coins for what they are worth. Put passion into it. Make it an affordable hobby.

✓ Remember that the evaluation, even if done by a professional service, is subjective... and subject to variations!

✓ Expect resellers to charge commissions (usually 20 percent on purchases or sales). To avoid excessive fees, however, find a reputable dealer and use a reputable coin price guide. For example, in the US, The Guidebook of US Coins, or The Red Book is best.

✓ If you're collecting together with a child, the best thing to do is probably to collect foreign coins, not all old ones. This way, you can combine knowledge of other cultures at the same time. You could also collect a country's last coin, as long as it wasn't taken out of circulation more than 500 years ago.

✓ To get hold of new coins for your collection, you can typically go to stock exchanges or collecting and numismatic halls. Social networks also offer different possibilities. I sometimes distrust the Internet because nothing looks more like a coin than another coin. In this case, the description and photos are really important to be sure of the quality of a coin and buy what you are really looking for. If you decide to buy on the Internet, choose collector sites such as Delcampe and professional sellers to avoid nasty surprises.

Do and don't

Do

✓ Increase your collection by going to coin exhibitions. You can also visit local retailers to look for bargains, and you can almost always find a cheap coin container suitable for both children and adults.

✓ Be patient: new collectors often feel the urge to have a complete coin set very quickly and as fast as they can. One of the things you should know is that the best coin collections are built over the course of many years.

✓ Note that some people recommend collecting out-of-circulation coins. A modern coin in circulation is typically only worth its face value, although there are exceptions to this rule.

✓ Do your research and specialize: the most successful coin collectors take time to learn as much as possible about numismatics and coins. So, you should not only study coins but the dynamics of the market as well. To learn more about coins, we suggest buying and reading as many books as possible about coins. So, you have to purchase books that address the theme of your collection.

✓ Try to understand the valuation of coins. Valuing coins is often difficult and people have a tendency to overvalue their coins. Also, be aware that the US grading system has higher prices than the UK, for example, a US coin valued at 'uncirculated' may be worth less than a coin valued at 'fine' in the UK.

Don'ts

✓ Do not expose the collection to substances or conditions that could deteriorate, oxidize, deform, etc.

✓ Always keep the collection in environments with stable temperature and humidity conditions.

- ✓ Gold coins don't need much care. Silver, bronze, copper or iron coins, on the other hand, are very sensitive to corrosion and humidity.
- ✓ Do not clean coins, especially with products that make them shine.
- ✓ Be careful when buying coins from online auctions. Unscrupulous sellers often overstate the value or condition of the coins. Also, there are frequent complaints about sellers not delivering coins.
- ✓ Avoid collecting ancient Chinese coins, as they are easy to imitate, and you would need to be a Chinese coin expert to determine if they are genuine.
- ✓ Avoid keeping coins in jars, shoe boxes, or most plastic containers. If the coins rub against each other, their value can go to zero. Additionally, some materials cause chemical reactions that can negatively affect the value of the coin.
- ✓ Polyvinyl chloride can damage coins. Over time, the green adhesive film, which can migrate from the container to the coin, can cause serious damage.
- ✓ Many times, when buying coins, some offers can be "too good to be true". Always inspect coins before buying and try to figure out if the coin is a counterfeit or a replica of the original. You may find out later when it comes to selling that the coin you thought was worth thousands is actually a copy or counterfeit.
- ✓ Realize that coins are speculative investments, that is, values (and prices) can go up or down.
- ✓ Periodically check the collection to prevent rust and deterioration, in order to notice it in time.

BOOK 4: ERRORS AND OTHER SPECIAL COINS GUIDE

Introduction

Here we are at the fourth guide of our fantastic journey into the world of coins. Specifically, we will talk about errors in coins, without forgetting other special coins guides.

This fourth guide will be divided into some really interesting chapters:

In the first chapter, you will find a complete guide for understanding error coins. We will talk about all of the relevance of error coins. So, we will understand why this relevance and errors are important, and why people collect error coins. There will also be a Classification and Type of errors. In the second chapter, we will show you how to identify an error coin: equipment and how, and frequently q&a.

In the third chapter, we will state some explanations in order to understand bullion coins: what is a bullion coin and why are important?

Chapter 4 will answer the question of whether you should invest in bullion coins or not. We will also deal with when to invest in bullion coins, since what year is not more used precious metal in the coins?

The final chapter is about understanding commemorative coins: what are and where to buy them.

CHAPTER 1: UNDERSTANDING ERROR COINS

2015, No mint Mark - Penny

Relevance of error coins

Know that that one penny coin you find at the bottom of your purse could turn out to be a treasure. The strange rules of numismatics, in fact, assign an astronomical value to all those coins that contain the so-called "minting error", i.e., a small detail that makes them rare and, on the luckiest occasions, even unique.

If you go to Ebay, for example, you can find 1-dollar coins sold for unthinkable amounts. Maybe you are tempted to think that all this is impossible but know right now that the price of a collectible coin is established on the basis of collectors' price lists which, as mentioned, primarily reward the uniqueness of the pieces.

In reality, as many collectors claim, there are thousands of coins in circulation with singular minting errors; the problem is that hardly anyone notices them and these unsuspected treasures pass from hand to hand without being identified. After all, to find them you would need an excellent magnifying glass and a lot of patience. Minting errors can be of various shapes, sizes or types. All these varieties of mistakes make collecting these coins fun and exciting.

Before starting to collect coins with minting errors, it is important to know which coins are, what types of errors are expected and above all to know the selling price of coins with errors like the one you are holding.

By minting varieties, we mean coins that have undergone graphic changes since their first issue. It can happen, for example, that a coin is issued and after a while, it is realized that a mistake has been made. The error is corrected by the engraver and a new contingent of coins is issued with the variant that corrects the error. It should be noted that in this case the coins with the error are not withdrawn and remain in circulation with legal tender. The errors that may vary may concern the symbol of the Mint, the initials of the engraver, a wrong design, the proportions of various parts of a coin, dates or alignments, improvements and more.

Minting errors are due to minting defects that have occurred unintentionally during the minting process of a coin. They are real errors and may be due to a minting defect due to deterioration during minting, such as weak minting pressure, lack of letters or numbers, off-centering, off-center image, deformity of the inside of the coin, breakage or wear of the punch or of part of it, double-sided coin, excess metal, or even coin smooth on both sides or one side only and more.

They could also be divided into two subcategories: minting errors due to errors due to the replacement of the minting and minting defects due to breakage, displacement and wear of the same. Among the most known minting errors are: Off Center, Clip, Wrong Flan, Clipped Edge, Double Value, Double Minting, Twins, Unconfined, Over Minting, Tired Minting, Double Hit, Double Head, Incused Image, Jump of Minting, Mule, Rotations Bimetallic with a single metal, blank shearing, excess minting.

It should be kept in mind that there are also coins with small differences in minting because when the punch is changed, this is never perfectly equal to the previous one.

This type of coin is not to be considered a mistake, but it is equally a piece to collect.

But why are collectors so attracted to coins with minting errors? Minting errors are an important aspect when evaluating a coin. The specimens with minting errors are generally rare coins whose demand is always very high.

Badly minted coins cannot be used to do anything. But apparently, they attract collectors from all over the world as a worthy addition to one's coin collection.

During the minting phase, coin producers usually eliminate most of the coins with minting errors. Some coins, however, escape controls and end up circulating daily and passing from hand to hand. And these coins, based on the minting error, can acquire an enormous value.

These coins very often far exceed their face value, and it all depends on the rarity or type of minting error.

In addition to the economic motivation, Mint coins also attract collectors due to their unusual appearance. Some coins with minting errors look quite strange. Mint coins have so many different flaws that, for the coin collector, you can put together a very impressive coin collection.

Classification of minting errors

There are essentially three broad categories of minting errors. These types of errors can also be found in all three simultaneously in the same coin.

Let's see in detail what these errors are:

- **Planchet errors**

The planchet is a rounded metal disc that contains the mixed alloys used to create a coin. Before the final minting takes place, the raw metal used to build it has the same shape as the planchet. The coin is then the appropriate shape and size, but it's just a piece of metal that hasn't been finished yet. In the case of normal coins, the metal plate has a raised edge and a well-rounded shape. The planchets are then struck and pressed, to create the definitive part of the future coin. Surely the question you are asking is how it is possible that a metal plate could be worth anything. The answer is given by the intrinsic value that the metal itself that is used to build the plate has.

Coin planchet errors vary based on certain factors. The price variations depending on the type of planchet, the date of minting, the type of minting error, the uniqueness of the error and the rarity of the planchet in circulation.

The most common errors that can be found in a planchet are:

- Planchet is completely smooth and without any imprinted elements
- The blow given to the planchet is completely off-center, in this case, the press partially hits the plate, causing the imprinted image to be off-center.
- Double blow, in this case, the coin is accidentally hit twice by the press and for this reason two identical and superimposed images are impressed.
- Cropped planchet, in this case, the error is in the cut of the plate, which has in any case undergone the pressing process but the size at this point is different from the original one.
- Planchets are addressed incorrectly, in this case, the plate intended for example for the minting of ten-cent coins is struck by the 50.

- **Die errors.**

The coin die is a hard piece of metal that is used to strike coins as they pass through the press for minting.

Nut errors occur either during the manufacture of the nut itself or, during use, due to the nut breaking or cracking.

- **Strike errors**

This category includes all types of errors that are linked to the physical part of the production of coins.

After talking about the broad categories that minting errors fall into, let's go on to see in detail what are the most common minting errors that you can find in coins.

Double die error

This error starts during the pressing process, but the error starts with the manufacturing of the die itself and not at the time the coin is minted. The second doubled die will have the same width and height as the original design and won't be flattened. That said, most coins with this type of error do not have high monetary values. However, if the doubling die error on the coin is rare and distinct, due to the popularity these coins have on the collector's market, then your coin will be worth a tidy sum of money.

It can happen that the hub hits the die in three different points of the coin and in this case, we will have a tripled die error, or it can hit the coins in four different points and in this case, we will have a quadrupled die error.

Die crack mint error

this is actually not a real mistake but a variety. The reason why it falls within the varieties and why different types of cracks have been discovered are all exactly the same. Since it is therefore a completely accidental printing change, this becomes a variety and not an error. In any case, it must also be specified that not all crepes are varieties. A die crack usually occurs when the stress on the die creates cracks in the face of the die. The cracks caused, however, are not deep, but mark the beginning of the end of the mold. The cracks in the coins give the coin itself little value but are used as indicators of variants known as PUPs or Pick Up Points.

Rim-to-rim die break cud

This type of failure is like die cracking, but more extensive, to the point where it can even cause the die to fall off. If the die failure goes from edge to edge, then it is called a CUD. Most die breaks are in the shape of a semi-circle and almost always occur at the edge of the coin.

Double or multiple-strike error

This type of error occurs when the coin being minted is struck two or more times before being released from the striking chamber.

This error occurs when the second shot is centered generating an overlap, either with the shot off-center or with both shots off-center. Coins with this type of error usually all look the same.

This type of error is very often combined with other minting errors.

Die cup mint error

This error occurs when the coin to be minted sticks to the hammer die. If the coin remains attached to the die for a long time, it will look like the cap of a bottle.

This type of error is defined as the king of minting errors because they are highly sought after by collectors and are resold or exchanged at fairly high prices compared to other types of minting errors. If the bottle cap that forms at the end of the minting is deep enough and has a well-defined shape, the coin can reach the value of 30,000 dollars. However, if you are not lucky enough to find this type of coin, be aware that most coins with the die cup mint error are usually valued between $2,000 and $3,000.

Broad strikes coin errors

This type of error occurs when the coin is minted outside its collar. The collar is the retaining ring that serves to indicate the precise final diameter that the coin that will then be minted must have. So, when a coin hits perfectly but lands off the collar it is called a Broadstrike. Furthermore, to fall into this type of error, the complete design of the coin must be present on both sides. When the coin is minted, the empty space that remains in the collar will widen, deforming itself on the outside, because the collar, when hit, will not be in the right position.

Multiple Strikes Inside the Collar Die

This type of error can be divided into two main categories: intentional and unintentional multiple strikes.

As far as intentional multiple strikes are concerned, proof coins or presentation pieces usually fall into this category of errors. These coins are struck intentionally many times inside the collar and usually have single images of excellent quality. The purpose of making these coins is to manually strike the coins several times to make the quality of the coin design better to appeal to collectors.

But often things don't go the right way and errors are created even during the controlled priming phase.

It happens instead that if the coin rotates between the various hits, then the hit coin will find itself having more images in the collar. The clearest image will be at the end of the various multiple shots, while the previous images will be mostly either erased or not very visible. Finding a coin with multiple rotated images is rare, but it happens to find some in circulation. Images with multiple strikes are more frequently found on proof coins, especially if the loose hammer die tilts or drifts off-center instead of rotating. In this way, the die will imprint more images superimposed on the coin and almost all these images will be on the same side.

Off-center struck coin

Coins that are struck off-center are certainly one of the most common and most recognizable minting errors in the world. This happens when a blank that should be immersed inside the press falls completely wrong on the collar. When the dies hit the blank incorrectly, then only that part will have the image of the coin imprinted on it. So, all off-center coins have a missing part of the design on one side of the coin. This missing part can be an inscription, the detail of the design or the dentils found on the edges of the coins.

Therefore, when a plate is not positioned correctly between the two dies, the result will be a coin with a partial design, if this design is missing completely then it is not an off-center strike.

When we talk about off-center struck you should know that the coin is described and evaluated based on the percentage of off-center with which the coin was minted. Where the planchet is positioned between the two dies when struck will determine the quality of the final missing design, and it is this percentage of off-center that will set the final price of the coin with the error. Off-center percentages usually range from 1 to 99%.

How do you go about determining the off-center percentage? Know that the amount of visible planchet is the key factor in determining the percentage. So, if 30% of the image is visible then the coin will be off-center by 30% and so on. The coins with the highest value, and therefore considered perfect for this type of error, are those that are off-center by 60%. The less visible the error, the lower the off-center percentage and the less value the coin has.

Basically, every set of coins that have been minted in the United States has some coin with one struck off-center. Some rare examples include some series that were minted for short periods of time or with extremely low mintages such as the Flying Eagle Cent, 20 Cent Piece and 3 Cent Silver.

Coins minted in more recent times have fewer rare off-center strikes than earlier ones. Most coins that were minted in the 1960s and coins like Lincoln Cents, Jefferson Nickels, and Washington

Quarters are often found off-center struck. Instead, what makes these coins more unique and valuable are the dates and the mint mark.

A complete rule of thumb you need to know to value off-center coins is based on size. In fact, according to this rule, the bigger the coin is the scarcer the error. This rule also applies to older coins. If you want to start collecting this type of coin with this type of errors, a good idea would be to form a collection made up of coins by mint date and mint mark, or a series of off-center coins, with a set of coins of the 20th century for each type of metal and design used for minting.

Partial collars errors

Partial collars are mint errors that occur when the impact press does not work properly. This way the collar will be in a completely wrong position and the lower die will get stuck in the collar. In this way, the final coin will have a strongly shaped edge.

As soon as the coin to be minted is struck, the lower die will lift upwards, and the struck coin will be pushed out of the collar.

If a blank is not positioned correctly, then it will end up with partial reeding after being hit. So, the coin will be found to have a partial cut and a surface that is partially hollow. The lower half of the coin shows the image while the upper edge part of the coin can be smooth or beveled or have both errors. Essentially, you can find three types of partial collar errors in a coin:

- Errors are known as rail edges, which are usually located on reed edges.
- Partial sloped collar errors were found in coins that have been minted with the plate sloped on the edge, causing uneven steps on the edges of the coin.
- Partial cartwheel collars occur on uncombed edges.
- Partial collar errors are quite common and less uncommon than off-center strikes or Broadstrikes errors.

Uniface Strikes

Coins with this type of error occur when two empty mint plates are inserted into the minting press at the same time. The empty space will hinder the work of the die both on the obverse side and on the reverse, thus preventing the design from being imprinted on the coin.

There are several coins that have this type of error. In addition to having the two sides of the coin completely empty, you can in fact find coins with minting outside the center or with an empty planchet in the collar. There are also coins that have one or more combinations of errors found on one face or side of the coin. Or there are uniface strikes due to the die cap being stuck to the die, striking blank planchets while taking the form of a die.

One of the most common errors of this type is the full uniface strike. This error occurs when one plate is perfectly centered on top of the other plate or when the two plates are hit at the same time. This error is also known as full indent.

When the chip or coin that is displaced from the center is struck by the chip below then the error is classified as an off-center uniface.

Indents

This type of coining error occurs when two blanks are inserted into the same collar and one of the two blanks is partially overlapped with the other.

When the hammer hits the coin, the blank which is placed on the top will be forced out by the blank which is placed on the bottom. This will create a sort of depression in the coin which is like that of the upper blank.

The indent can be found on both the obverse and the reverse of the coin and can occur on the first or second strike. The coin can also be minted with indentations also inside and outside of the coin.

Bonded Coins

This type of error is created when the feeder system, which supplies the blank planchets to the press, malfunctions or jams. In this case, the minted coin is not ejected properly and another planchet is inserted into the collar and struck while the previous coin is still there. By doing so, the two coins will crush and be fused together.

The bonded error process can occur multiple times as more coins are inserted and bonded together. When you have a stack of coins tied together then it is called pin-up-bonded.

One of the most iconic coins with this type of error is the Lincoln cent which was struck on three copper and zinc axes in an irregular manner.

Mated Pairs

The mated pairs error occurs when two individual coins, which already have different errors, are minted together. Mated pair errors come in many shapes and sizes.

For example, mated pairs can occur when a coin is hit off-center while on top of another coin. Another type of error occurs when a blockage is found on a coin that has already been minted and perfectly centered but is struck again by mistake.

The rarest type of this type of error occurs when two die caps, i.e., straight and reverse, are closed at the same time and both dies are coupled.

Mated pairs can also be found in an off metal, i.e., when a smaller blank planchet, or a smaller already minted coin, is minted on top of another coin with larger dimensions.

This type of error is extremely rare and, the most emblematic example, is the mated pairs between a Franklin Half mated with a Lincoln cent.

Fold-Over Strikes

A fold-over strike is one of the most drastic errors to be found in a coin. This type of error occurs when the blank is placed vertically between the two dies. When the coin is struck, the force is so great that it bends and folds the piece of metal that is supposed to be the future coin. Furthermore, during the mold, the planchet or coin can enter the beating chamber and then rotate on the edge.

Or, if the planchet which is vertically oriented is moved to the periphery of the striking chamber, then the coin will bend either outward or inward.

These coin folds can be found both centered and off-centered and can usually be found in various shapes and sizes.

CHAPTER 2: HOW TO IDENTIFY AN ERROR COIN

Minting errors can vary from coin to coin and can be simple and trivial errors or be more evident and significant.

If you want to become an expert and understand minting errors, without having to resort to the opinion of an expert, you must pay attention to 6 types of errors that are very common and easily identifiable.

- Inscription error: most of the errors you find in coins are basically found in the inscriptions. Often, the most common lettering errors are missing letters or doubling of letters. Doubling is usually only found in one part of a single word.

- Date and mint mark error. This type of error is rarer than the previous ones. For this reason, coins with these errors have a significantly high value. In this case, you will have to pay attention to reprinted dates or mint marks, or to excessive punching, or doubling of dates or letters.

- Errors on the primary element. These types of errors are easy to spot as they are always found on the image embossed in the coin. In this case, all you need to do is check both sides of the coin and look for something out of the ordinary, such as a doubling or missing elements in the image. This type of error gives a high value to the coin in question.

- Errors in the use of materials. There are some coins that do not have any kind of visible error but have defects in the use of the creation material, which is different from the standard one. To understand this error, just read carefully what materials the various types of coins are made of and learn to identify the differences by sight.

- Matrix rotation errors. These errors can be identified by the rotation of the elements that are on the opposite side of the coin. Look at the face of the coins and then make sure it is always facing up. Then turn the coin over and make sure that the elements on this side of the coin are also facing up. If one or more elements do not follow this pattern, then you are in the presence of a rotation error. Most coins with rotation errors are easy to spot. Also, coins that have large offsets may have moderate value, unless you get lucky and find coins with offsets of around 180° then the value of the coin will go up significantly.

- Errors on the edge of the coin. Many errors in the coins are found along the edges. You can try twirling the coin in your hand so that you can feel if the coin has any spots that aren't even. Mistakes to pay particular attention to are lines, or missing edges, or edge stitching. You should also check for doubling of letters or missing letters along the edges.

The equipment needed to find minting errors

That said, to be able to find errors in the coins you plan to collect, you need to equip yourself with special equipment. Even if it is true that many errors are visible even at first glance, equipping yourself with specific equipment for searching for errors will be useful.

The elements you absolutely must not do without are:

- A magnifying glass is better if it is the one used by jewelers or even better if you manage to equip yourself with a digital microscope. In fact, as far as magnifier power is concerned a 10x power would be ideal, but magnifiers with 7x power can also be used and you will get decent results. However, remember that the 7X power is the absolute minimum value that you will need to consider.
- A desk lamp.
- A piece of cloth will help you clean the surfaces of the coins well.
- A coin collector, with divided compartments where you can put the coins you want to collect.

FAQ

What is Cherrypicking?

Cherrypicking is an approach widely used by collectors and hunters of coins containing errors. The process of Cherrypicking involves picking a group of coins and carefully and repeatedly examining them one at a time.

Is there a way to sort the Minting coins correctly?

A fundamental rule to having your collection of Minting coins well organized is to put them in order according to denomination. This will make it easier for you to check all your coins and it will also make the bug-hunting process easier, as you will more easily notice any subtle discrepancies between each coin.

What should I look for in a coin to understand if there is an error?

Some coins with minting errors have a high value compared to others. If the error is difficult to find even with a high-power magnifier, then this error is minor and therefore your coin will be worth very little. Usually, the most important things to check are the inscriptions on the obverse of the coin, the images on the coin, the reverse and edges of the coin, and the inscriptions on the coin.

CHAPTER 3: UNDERSTANDING BULLIONS COINS

Bullion coins are essentially coins produced using precious metals. They are minted in weights that are a fraction of a troy ounce, and the material most used for their production is gold and often silver, although sometimes platinum or palladium pieces are made.

Many countries in the world have their own collection of official bullion coins, such as the American Eagle which is the official series of gold coins of the United States.

Gold or Bullion coins are a form of payment that has existed in practice for thousands of years. In fact, these coins have been used as a primary form of payment for much of history. After the advent of the fiat currency system, the role of these coins has changed considerably, and their use is now relegated to a collector's item or an investment form.

Bullion coins are mainly issued by government agencies of the various countries they belong to, however, there are some rare cases where these coins are minted by private agencies.

As we said, bullion coins are coins made up almost entirely of precious metals, we speak of 90% or more of purity, and the quantity of metal used for minting is shown on the coin itself. The amount of metal to be used is established based on a standard metric and furthermore, you will also find the name of the agency that created the coin stamped on the coin.

Bullion coins can be purchased either from the government agency or from institutions that print coins, provided there are supplies available.

Most of these coins have a limited edition, and very often the supply of these precious coins runs out quickly. In this way, all that remains is the secondary market where they can be purchased, i.e., from private owners, or from other coin collectors or coin dealers.

CHAPTER 4: SHOULD YOU INVEST IN BULLION COINS?

Among the various forms of investment available, the purchase of valuable coins, first in gold, is one of the most loved by a well-defined subject: the collector. Behind the passion for bullion coins, there is not only the goal of making a profit, but also the love for an object that has always tickled the imagination and the search for the rarest and most precious piece.

For coin collectors, bullion coins are highly sought after and appreciated due to their rarity, but also for their beauty from a purely aesthetic point of view. These two elements, especially if they are concomitant, can greatly increase the value of the coin, regardless of the type of precious metal with which it was made.

This completely subjective value is known as the numismatic value of bullion coins. The value that is attributed to these coins only for the precious material with which they were made is known as melting value.

If your aim is not only to collect but also to use these coins as a form of investment, then the advice is to buy bullion coins and use them as a hedge against inflation. The reason they serve as a buffer in the event of inflation is that their value increases as the purchasing power of fiat currencies decreases.

Bullion coins can also be risk hedges for areas such as currency trading or traditional equities. Usually, when those who invest decide to buy precious metals, such as silver, platinum or gold, it is done to have a safe entry in case the markets collapse, and traditional shares fall to the bottom. Precious metals, in fact, always go in the opposite direction compared to economic performance, i.e., they greatly increase their value if the rest of the economy goes badly. In this way, if you have chosen to base your investment portfolio on shares based only on economic growth, with the billions of coins you will compensate for any losses. Then when the market starts to rise again, then those who invest in this material asset can decide to sell to make a good profit.

One of the questions that the neophyte of the sector asks himself the most is the following: what is the best investment coin? Of course, this question is generated by the desire to invest with the greatest possible security, so as not to incur capital losses.

The truth is that the smartest thing to do, before proceeding with the actual purchase, is to get a good general understanding of the sector. Today with the Internet it is not difficult, a quick search is enough to find the sites where it is possible to buy investment coins and then deepen the search by evaluating the value of the individual pieces by reading the many forums available where crowds of collectors and passionate investors exchange their opinions. After you have everything clear, then you can proceed with your first purchase of bullion coins.

However, there are certainly some coins that are particularly appreciated and therefore can be considered among the best investment in bullion coins available on the market.

- American Eagle (United States). Distinguished by the famous image of the eagle symbol of America, the American Eagle is the most significant bullion coin of the United States of America. It has a face value of 50 dollars and has always been considered one of the best investment gold coins from the point of view of the protection of the invested capital in the medium and long term. It is issued in 22 carats, therefore with a degree of purity 916.7/1000, and is available in four denominations: 1oz, 1/10oz, 1/4oz and 1/2oz. The American Eagle certainly represents a safe investment, not only for the solidity, credibility and weight on the global scenario of the issuer, all important things when it comes to bullion coins, but also thanks to the fact that it is traded in large quantities every day. In short, it is an extremely popular gold coin that can be useful, especially in smaller denominations, to diversify and secure the investment portfolio of a small saver. A very good thing about this coin is that it can be liquidated at any time you want. We are also talking about an object with quite a lot of history behind it: the first American gold coin was minted in 1795 and was worth 10 dollars, while the first investment coin was issued in 1986. It is produced in two versions: Proof and uncirculated. The proof is a particularly valuable issue intended primarily for collectors. Uncirculated instead means that the coin is in perfect condition, therefore that it is brand new or that it has been perfectly preserved and does not show any visible damage.

- Vienna Philharmonic (Austria). Those who are passionate about classical music cannot fail to know one of the most famous and renowned orchestras in the world: the Vienna Philharmonic, which gives its name to this bullion coin. The coin portrays the world-famous Great Organ of the Philharmonic and the instruments of the Musikverein. Issued for the first time in 1989, it is famous for its beauty and is absolutely one of the best-selling and most appreciated investment coins in the world. It was the first coin of its kind to be issued with a face value in euros, while until 2002 it was minted in shillings. Also called Phili, it is still today among the best-selling bullion coins in the world and in addition to the gold one, the silver and platinum versions are also issued. It is a pure gold coin, therefore 999.9/1000 (24 carats) and has kept its design unchanged from 1989 to today. Of course, due to its popularity, the Vienna Philharmonic can certainly be ranked among the best investment bullion coins. Easily liquidated, it is enjoying increasing success in emerging markets, first of all, the Chinese one, but it has always been among the most popular in North America, Japan and Europe.

- Britannia (United Kingdom). The Britannia was the first European bullion gold coin and is a legal tender in Great Britain. It is also famous because in the United Kingdom, it is exempt from Capital Gain Tax, in practice no taxes are paid on the proceeds of the sale, and therefore it is considered an excellent investment to guarantee a tax-free profit. Minted in pure 24-karat gold, it represents an excellent opportunity for those who want to invest in gold coins, also thanks to its well-known liquidity. It is important to underline that 24 carats were introduced in issues from 2013 onwards, while previously it was gold with 916.7 degrees of purity, therefore 22 carats. The design impressed on both faces, very refined and appreciated by both investors and collectors, is made with advanced minting techniques which make the Britannia very safe from the point of view of every possible counterfeiting, as is well known to any expert in the sector. On the market, the Britannia issued in past years continue to have very interesting prices and this coin has always represented a safe haven for anyone who wants to introduce elements of diversification into their investment portfolio. The face value of the 1oz Britannia is £100, although, of course, the real market value is much higher.

- China Panda. The China Pandas are characterized by a peculiarity: every year the design is renewed, but always with the same elements, and this makes the Chinese gold investment coin a favorite among collectors, as well as investors naturally, precisely because of the design customized for each year of issue, a feature that increases the numismatic value of the China Panda. Furthermore, each issue is characterized by numerically limited production, so much so that it is customary to book your purchase to avoid being sold out. A curiosity of the China Panda: the images on the front and back are reversed depending on whether the coin is distributed on the national or international market. Another peculiarity of the China Panda is that since 2016 production no longer takes place in ounces but with the metric system. The Chinese bullion coin is 24-karat gold and is also minted in silver, palladium and platinum.

- Pound (United Kingdom). The Gold Sovereign, the real name of this well-known UK gold bullion coin, has a face value of one pound and is 22 carats. Of course, it is also offered in other denominations, not just the one pound. There are various types, and the value is determined by a long series of factors: new and old minting, the quantity of gold, or the state of conservation. Those who want to invest in precious coins can also find the gold pound in the bank, but it is good to do your own accounts and understand whether it is convenient to buy it from a credit institution, given that it is possible to buy the investment gold pound on one of the many online services available, without intermediaries of any kind. Generally, these sites, which buy and sell, therefore in addition to selling investment coins they buy them, carry out shipments with couriers specialized in this kind of service, therefore in total safety. Consider that in general the investment Sovereigns of the old minting, therefore before 1957, are worth a little less than those of the new minting. In general, the value of this coin is mainly determined by its weight and therefore by the quantity of gold present, but some issues also have a numismatic quotation, therefore greater than the simple value of the gold they are made of. Sovereigns with a numismatic value, as for all other coins, are those where there is a minting error, or if the issue was in a limited series, or if the issue date corresponds to a particularly significant historical event. Among the most important gold Sovereigns ever produced, we find that of the 2017 issue, minted when the anniversary of the first issue of the so-called Modern Sovereign. These coins, the ones produced in 2017, have wonderful shield-shaped punching. Given its history and obviously the prestige of the issuing country, the gold pound is to be considered absolutely one of the best investment coins on the market. Being 22 carats, it is composed of an alloy of gold and copper, with the latter giving the investment Sovereign its characteristic color that distinguishes it.

- Krugerrand (South Africa). It is the first gold bullion coin that is easily accessible, essentially for the retail market, and which has therefore paved the way for other products of the same type. It was first minted in 1967 and is, of course, one of the most popular bullion gold coins in the world. It should be noted that the South African Krugerrand has no nominal monetary value, and its valuation practically corresponds to the gold quotation. It is in fact commonly used to legally exchange it for the cash equivalent of its weight in gold. Its success has always been a point of reference, just think that in 1980 the South African Krugerrand represented 80% of the sales of 1-ounce gold investment coins. It is not a pure gold coin; in fact, it is 22 carats (916.7 in terms of purity) and is characterized by a reddish color that comes from the presence of copper in the alloy. Among investors, this coin is particularly appreciated for the refinement of the design and obviously, for the history, it can boast, representing in fact an icon of investment coins. The 2017 version should be mentioned, which celebrated the 50th anniversary of the first issue of the South African Krugerrand.

- Maple Leaf (Canada). Absolutely among the most traded investment coins on the market, the Maple Leaf is characterized by the characteristic maple leaf symbol of Canada. The first Gold Maple Leaf was struck in 1979. The Royal Mint of Canada produced the gold Maple Leaf in 1979 to enter the 1-ounce gold coin market, at that time dominated by the South African Krugerrand, which however was boycotted by other countries due to the regime of apartheid in South Africa. The Canadian Gold Maple Leaf has a strong national connotation, the maple leaf is in fact the symbol of Canada and is also present on the national flag. Furthermore, the coin is made up only of gold extracted from Canadian mines. On the market, it is universally recognized as one of the most beautiful and prestigious gold coins, also because it was practically the first to be minted with a purity of 99.9%, therefore at 24 carats. Its weight corresponds exactly to 1 troy ounce or 31.10 grams. Its diameter is 30 millimeters, while its face value is 50 Canadian dollars. The thickness is equal to 2.93 mm.

- Kangaroo (Australia). With a name clearly inspired by the animal symbol of Australia, this gold investment coin, also called Nugget (nugget), from 1986, the year of its debut on the market and until 1989, represented a nugget. In subsequent issues, a red kangaroo was instead depicted, considered more representative of the country. Made in 24 carats, it is distinguished by its limited edition and the fact that every year it is minted with a new motif. These two specific characteristics, added to the different formats available of the Australian Kangaroo Nugget, the limited edition and the refinement of the minting make this bullion coin one of the most appreciated by collectors and one of the most fascinating coins in the coin collecting market.

- Marengo (Italia). It is loved by collectors, not just Italians. Marengo was issued for the first time in 1801 to celebrate the French victory over the Austrians the previous year and for this reason, it is also called Napoleon. Regarding the issues of the Italian state, it was minted from 1861 to 1923, but not continuously. The Marengo is therefore a gold investment coin, 21.6 carats, with a strong numismatic value, due to the concomitance with important historical events and the rarity of the coins belonging to particular issues. Naturally, there are different types, also issued by other States during the so-called Latin Monetary Union (Belgium, Austria, Switzerland, France) but the Marengo Vittorio Emanuele II has particular value, the first issued by the Italian State (the next one shows the effigy of Humbert I).

Pros and cons of investing in bullion coins

Let's see a summary of the advantages and disadvantages of buying bullion coins, obviously with a particular eye to gold ones, which are the most requested and sought-after on the market.

Let's see first why investing in bullion coins is convenient:

- They are not subject to VAT taxation in many countries.
- They are independent of stock and financial market fluctuations.
- Excellent coverage from collapses of government bonds.
- A perfect solution to diversify your investment portfolio.
- Immediate liquidity.
- They are negotiable between individuals.
- They are easily stored.

The subject of very fast liquidity is perhaps the most important fact for the small saver, also because it must be considered a fact: investing in bullion coins, in gold or other precious metals, allows you to dispose of only a part of the investment if you need liquidity. It is true that today it is possible to buy even small gold bars, but managing the coins is certainly easier and more convenient.

Another advantage to take into consideration is the convenience of storing coins that can be kept at home, possibly in a safe. It is certainly more convenient to have 500 one-ounce gold coins each than a bar that weighs 500 ounces.

The cons of investing in bullion coins are very few:

- Slight surplus at the time of purchase compared to the price of the precious metal.
- A minimum of industry knowledge is required.
- Any damage to the coin will result in a decrease in its value.

Another disadvantage to taking into consideration is that it is necessary to pay a slight surcharge compared to the purchase of an ingot of the same weight since the price of investment coins is higher than the equivalent of the precious metal due to production costs, storage and of transport. But it's actually not really a disadvantage as you can recoup this markup when you sell the coins, and this markup falls on the buyer.

In short, as we have seen in this chapter, bullion coins, especially gold ones, are an excellent safe haven for those who want to secure their capital from the whims of the financial economy in which, like it or not, we live, and also to diversify your investment portfolio.

You need little knowledge, a little attention to follow the quotations of precious metals to buy at the right time, care of the coins to always keep them in mint condition and not to make them lose value and above all be careful to buy the best ones, therefore the most requested by investors and collectors. In this way, it will be easier to resell them and immediately realize the desired liquidity.

CHAPTER 5: UNDERSTANDING COMMEMORATIVE COINS

Commemorative coins are special coins that are produced by individual states to celebrate themes or events. They are minted with a distinctive design that refers to the particular event for which they were issued.

Most of these coins are issued for collecting purposes, although some countries also use these coins in regular monetary circulation.

A large part of these coins for commemorative purposes is issued every year, in order to underline the importance of some historical personalities, culture, traditions, monuments or archaeological sites of the countries in which they are issued.

The function of these coins is to be ambassadors of the countries of origin, and they are objects that last over time, evoking memories of certain special events in the minds of the people who own them.

Many countries currently produce commemorative coins as a very pleasant and beautiful way to get noticed by the rest of the world.

What makes these coins different from normal coins in circulation is the fact that only a precise number of them are produced, they are minted only for a short period of time before the mint withdraws the coinage and the original coins are used again.

Another interesting aspect of commemorative coins is that when they are minted, not only coins are produced at that time, but also traditional coins are produced. Therefore, both types of coins are put into circulation at the same time and will all have the same issue date.

Alongside commemorative coins, commemorative coins are often minted for the purpose of raising funds. These coins are produced in limited editions to be sold directly to coin collectors and the price at which they are sold is much higher than their face value. The reason why they are paid more is therefore not due to the preciousness of the coin but to the rarity of these coins.

The first commemorative coin of the United States was born in 1892, and the purpose of the coin was to commemorate the World Columbian Exposition.

1892 marked the beginning of the production of commemorative coins and since then several coins have been minted and issued for commemorative purposes. The coins were usually minted with precious metals, such as gold and silver, and their purpose was to commemorate interest groups who influenced Congress in one way or another. The era of commemorative coins in the United States ended in 1954.

However, in 1982, the minting of commemorative coins resumed with the release of the 250th anniversary of George Washington's birth commemorative coin. The coin was minted on a half-dollar piece and from this time began a new era of commemorative coin production in the United States. All commemorative coins minted after 1982 fall into the modern-era commemorative coin category. Despite the minting of modern-era commemorative coins, these coins also reverted to having the same problems as the earlier coins. In fact, only coins were issued that supported the interests of small groups and that served to help causes of interest to a few people.

For this reason, in 1998 Congress enacted a law that prevents the minting of commemorative coins above a certain pre-established number.

Types of commemorative coins

Regardless of the country from which they come, there are 3 main types of commemorative coins:

- Common everyday currency coins are commemorative coins that are minted on coins that are in normal active circulation. Like normal circulation coins, these coins are also made of the same materials used for traditional coins.

- Non-circulating legal tender, are commemorative coins that derive from old coins which are then melted down. The metals used for minting are either basic metals or precious metals. Theoretically, these coins could circulate like normal coins, but it is quite disadvantageous since the collectible value is higher than their legal tender issue price.

- Tokens and souvenirs, are regarded as proof of commemorative coins and are minted from precious metals. This type of coin is not legal tender and, since they are created in a limited edition, they are the most valued and sought after by collectors.

Where are commemorative coins produced?

Physical coins are created by the Mint of the various states. Then they are minted in the same place where the coins normally used by the various states are minted.

The production process of commemorative coins is the same as that used for the production of ordinary coins.

In the United States, the responsibility for designing and then creating these commemorative coins rests with Congress.

The design of the specific commemorative coin is then carried out by the organization or groups that will benefit from it.

What is the value of commemorative coins?

As far as the evaluation of commemorative coins is concerned, it must be said immediately that there is no universal rule that can be applied to all coins.

As we said in the introductory part of this chapter, in general, the value of a commemorative coin goes up according to the material of production and the rarity of the coin.

Furthermore, non-circulating commemorative coins are highly sought after by collectors not only for their beauty and rarity but above all for their high economic value.

When it comes to valuing a commemorative coin, experts take the following aspects into consideration:

- The condition of the coin.
- The year it was minted.
- Minting errors.
- The value of bullion coins in real-time.

It should also be emphasized that on a technical level, commemorative coins are legal tender just like ordinary ones. however, since their value is higher than the nominal one, it would be inadvisable to spend them as if they were ordinary coins. If you decide to use them to pay for your commemorative coins, they will certainly be accepted but their value will be equal to that of coins that are in regular circulation, therefore a 1-dollar commemorative coin will have a value of 1 dollar. The value of these coins only goes up the moment you decide to sell them to dealers or coin collectors. For this reason, good advice is not to spend these coins but to keep them, to obtain a good profit once you decide to sell them to competent personnel.

The best commemorative coins to collect

Below you will find the list of the most beautiful and significant commemorative coins in the world:

- 2-euro coin minted in 2007 to commemorate the 25th anniversary of the death of Princess Grace: in 2007, a commemorative 2-euro coin was issued by the Principality of Monaco, dedicated to the 25th anniversary of Grace Kelly's death, with a circulation of 20,000 pieces. The coin can reach a valuation of 3,000 euros and more.

- 2-euro BU commemorative coin dedicated to the 100th anniversary of the coronation of Our Lady of Meritxell as patroness of the Principality of Andorra. Featured on this beautiful commemorative coin is the sculpture of Our Lady of Meritxell, who is the patroness of the Principality of Andorra, dating back to the 11th and 12th centuries. The patron saint is the symbol of the identity of the Andorran people and is a source of passion and pride for the inhabitants of Andorran. On the background of the coin is a reproduction of the sanctuary of the basilica where the intaglio is found, a graphic element symbolizing a flower, the name of the issuing country "ANDORRA" and the years "1921-2021". The twelve stars of the European flag appear on the ring of the coin. The limited edition consists of 70,000 copies in numbered coin cards.

- Peace commemorative dollar of 1921. The coin was minted in 1921 and remained in circulation until 1928, then in 1934 and 1935 and finally in 1921. It was designed by Anthony de Francisci, after winning a competition to find the most emblematic images to represent peace. The obverse of the coin depicts the head and neck of the Goddess of Liberty in profile, while the reverse features a bald eagle clutching an olive branch, with the inscription Peace. This commemorative one-dollar coin is to be minted for circulation using silver as the base metal. In 2012, the United States Mint began issuing the 2021 Peace Dollar to celebrate the 100th anniversary of the minting of the first coin. The minting of these coins will continue from 2023 onwards.

- The Gold Standard 2021 UK Quarter-Ounce Gold Proof Coin. For the first time, the Gold Standard is commemorated in a coin. The coins were minted in 2021, are quarter-ounce coins and feature scales, designed by Royal Mint designer, Dominique Evans. The coin design is completed with the portrait of Elizabeth II and Jody Clark. Jody Clark appears on the obverse of the coin with an inscription indicating the face value of the coin which is £25. The minting of this coin is very limited, in fact, only 500 specimens were produced.

BOOKS 5: COIN COLLECTING IN THE WORLD

Introduction

As we have seen in previous books, coin collecting can be considered either a hobby or have economic or commercial goals and objectives.

Collectors love to collect coins that were used or minted in ancient times.

Coin collecting, especially old or rare coins, is also a lucrative form of investment. The increase in disposable income in some families and the interest in antiques have also increased the sales of collector coins in all parts of the world.

Therefore, considering all these positive factors, forecasts say that the world coin-collecting market will witness exponential growth over time.

Geographically, we can divide the coin-collecting market into 5 main areas: North America, Europe, Asia and the entire Pacific area, the Middle East and Africa and finally Latin America.

Even if the primacy of collecting is held by the United States of America, current forecasts see this hobby growing more and more in the European market.

CHAPTER 1: TOP COINS COLLECTS AS BEGINNERS

It can be difficult to know where to start or what to collect, especially if you're just starting out. In any case, if you happen to have a handful of coins in your wallet or in your home stored as a safe haven, you can probably already be considered a coin collector.

Some of you may have been given commemorative coins in your lifetime, while others still have a handful of foreign coins from overseas holidays or from their leisure or business trips.

Now, the next step is to think about what types of coins you like the most and whether you want to collect them. Many people simply decide to collect coins that relate to a historical period they like to learn more about. Or, if you're not too interested in a particular period of history, you might want to collect commemorative coins for special historical events.

A very useful tip, regardless of the type of coin or coins you want to collect, is to buy a coin folder to keep all your coins clearly visible and in one place. These are available at coin collectors' fairs, as well as major online shopping portals. They are also not too expensive and are extremely useful.

A typical collection of coins is one with exhibition points where 2 or 3 coins are inserted, however, the most beautiful and complete are those that have an assortment of coins of various shapes and different sizes.

Top USA coins to collect

Below you will find a list of the most popular US coins.

Lincoln Penny

They are great coins if you are on your first coin collection. The reason is that these coins were minted in large quantities, so they are easy to both find and buy at a low price.

To go more specifically, the Lincoln Head Copper Penny, minted in 1943 is a coin that you can easily find and that is collected by many coin enthusiasts.

Kennedy Half Dollar

It is certainly one of the most popular coins among coin collectors. The coin was first minted in 1964 to commemorate President John F. Kennedy following his assassination in 1963.

Mintage of the Kennedy half a dollar began in 1964 and continues to this day; 1964 was done in two mints and silver, 1965 to 1970 was done cuprous/nickel plated, 1971 to present plated and silver, 1976 was done to commemorate the bicentennial with Independence Hall.

Wheat cents

They are highly sought after and prized by coin collectors. The reason is the easy availability of these coins and the low purchase price because they were minted in very large quantities.

The coin was designed by sculptor Victor Brenner under commission from the US Mint in 1908. The coin was to celebrate the centennial of Abraham Lincoln's birth and therefore his image was to be featured on the coin. This was also, for this reason, one of the first circulating coins to have the imprinted image of a president.

The coin was minted in 95% copper. That was until 1943 when copper was replaced by galvanized steel for a year. In 1944 some coins with errors were minted, i.e., the coins were minted on steel planchets, and these coins, in addition to being rare, also have a high economic value.

The original copper composition returned to us in 1959 and the grain design was replaced with Frank Gasparro's reverse design of the Lincoln Memorial.

In the new coin design, there is an image of Lincoln facing right on the obverse of the coin, while on the reverse there are two stalks of wheat tying around the edge of the coin framing the words ONE CENT and UNITED STATES OF AMERICA. On the upper edge of the coin is the motto E PLURIBUS UNUM.

1921 Peace Dollar

In 1921, at the end of the First World War, eight American artists were commissioned to present the design of the new silver dollar which was supposed to celebrate and symbolize world peace. The victor, Anthony de Francisci created a coin with an image of Liberty printed on the obverse and a print of a bald eagle holding an olive branch and sitting on a mountain on the reverse. the reverse of the coin also features the sunrise to symbolize a new day of peace and freedom for the whole world. These dollars were minted from 1921 to 1928 and from 1934 to 1935. This dollar is the last silver dollar minted in the United States.

Top Worldwide coins to collect

Below you will find a list of the most beautiful and valuable collectible coins in the world.

The silver money of emperor Adrian

The silver denarius depicting the great Emperor Hadrian weighs approximately 3.8 g, has a diameter of approximately 18 mm, and is usually found in a good state of conservation. On the obverse is the emperor Hadrian with a laurel branch facing right; on the reverse is the allegorical figure of Pietas.

Silver taler of maria Theresa of Hapsburg

The silver thaler of Maria Theresa of Habsburg is one of the most collected coins in the world and was minted in Austria on several occasions between 1780 and 1950.

Maria Theresa of Habsburg governed her country for four decades, earning the nickname of "mother of Europe" since two of her 11 daughters became queens: Marie Antoinette, the last queen of France, and Maria Carolina, queen of the two Sicilies.

The coin has a weight of 28.06 g and a diameter of 41.00 mm, and the metal used for minting is 833 silver.

Vatican, the silver of pope John Paul II

On 16 October 1978, the cardinals gathered in a conclave and chose the Pole Karol Wojtyla as the new pontiff. The first non-Italian Pope after 455 years, Wojtyla chose the name of John Paul II.

In his 26 years of pontificate, he toured the world several times, reaching the last of all continents and giving a more modern image of the Roman Church. Wojtyla became a true icon, a public figure whose face has been imprinted on T-shirts and flags and obviously on coins.

This 500 Lire silver coin immortalizes the face of the Pope and the Cross of Christ, and over time has become one of the most iconic issues among those of the Vatican. Made of 835 silvers, it weighs 11 g and has a diameter of 29.1 mm.

The 25 pence of the royal wedding between Charles and Diana

The 25p coin of Prince Charles and Diana Spencer was issued in 1981 by Great Britain to celebrate the royal wedding.

The married couple is portrayed in profile, contrasted with the unforgettable Queen Elizabeth II depicted on the opposite face.

The beautiful coin is made of cupronickel, has a diameter of 38 mm and a weight of 30 gr.

Low budget collection

As we said at the beginning of this chapter, you are new to collecting and you want to start your own collection, but you don't know where to start. Furthermore, being at the beginning, you don't even want to spend a fortune on your new passion.

Numismatics is a fun and exciting hobby but at the beginning, it can be demotivating both because many pieces are really hard to find and because some coins are really expensive, especially for those on a limited budget.

To help you in your hobby, we are going to list some collectible coins that can be purchased and collected on a budget of less than $100.

Nickel Jefferson

The Jefferson nickel was first minted in 1938 after the US Treasury decided to substitute it for the Buffalo nickel. The Buffalo nickel, also known as Indiana head nickel, had completed its circulation cycle, which lasted a total of 25 years, and the new president of the United States, Roosevelt, decided to have a coin minted with the effigy of one of the presidents he particularly admired: Thomas Jefferson.

The 5-cent coin was designed by Felix Schlag, a German immigrant who had arrived in the United States in 1929.

On the obverse of the coin, there is a portrait of President Jefferson that the designer had found in an art book done by Gilbert Stuart, while on the reverse of the coin Monticello is depicted. When first minted in 1938, this coin remained unchanged for 66 years.

Even if the images have remained unchanged, the variations suffered by the coin have mainly been at the level of the metal used for its minting. For most of the coin's history, the metal content was an alloy of 75% copper and 25% nickel. During the Second World War, due to the use of metals for the manufacture of weapons, the metal content of this coin underwent a drastic change and became 56% copper, 35% silver and 9% manganese.

If you want to start a low-budget collection with this type of coins in total, you should assemble 176 coins. Most of these coins, being that the Jefferson nickel is still in circulation as ordinary money, you will find in your wallet, or you can go to a bank even locally and buy rolls of Jefferson nickel. The only difficulty will be in finding the coins that were minted in wartime, i.e., those ranging from 1942 to 1945. Once you have collected most of the common and low-cost coins, you can do a quick calculation and buy 1 or 2 of that historical periods to complete your collection.

State quarters collections

This is one of the most well-known and collected coin sets in the United States. The 50 State Quarters coin program, implemented by the United States Mint, began in 1999 and lasted a total of 10 years. The purpose of these commemorative coins was to celebrate each state that is part of the country, scheduling the minting according to the order in which the state upheld the Constitution or was added to the Union. The coins were created every 3 months and after 10 years they have not been reproduced and will not be reproduced again.

However, these coins are still in circulation, and you are likely to find them easily in your wallet.

Furthermore, the coins, given their wide distribution on the market, have a fairly low price which corresponds, in practice, to their nominal value which is 25 cents.

However, there are also uncirculated sets, which have a slightly higher price but which, if you can find them in a coin shop, would not affect your budget, making your collection more complete and with a higher value than the use of only 50 classic coins.

CHAPTER 2: RAREST COINS IN THE WORLD

When we talk about coins that are worth a fortune, we mean rare and precious ones, which are considered unique collector's items. But it is important that these are in an excellent state of conservation, to increase their value.

Another factor that is considered is circulation, i.e., the rarer a coin is, the higher its value. The level of rarity is evaluated based on the quantity of that piece in circulation, as well as the date of issue. Very often you are in possession of small fortunes without knowing it, so it is always advisable to check your coins carefully and regularly.

But getting to the heart of the matter, which are the rarest and most valuable coins in the world?

If you are wondering which are the rarest and most precious coins in the world, in this chapter they will be described in detail.

Flowing Hair Silver Dollar

At the top of the list is the flowing-haired dollar minted in 1794, which has exceeded 10 million dollars in value. It was the first coin issued by the federal government of the United States, and it is a small silver coin minted in the first American Mint opened in Philadelphia. Its value hit the record during a public auction that took place at Stack's Bowers Galleries in New York City on January 24, 2013.

Double Eagle

In 1933, American President Roosevelt gave the order to destroy the 1933 gold Double Eagle series, over 445,000 copies of 20 American dollars.

The Double Eagle is one of the most precious coins not only in American history and has an incredible story behind it: it is the last gold coin minted by the US Mint (in fact it marks the exit of the United States from the gold exchange standard), it is part of a series that never entered circulation, it has passed through prestigious private collections (from the Egyptian king Farouk to the New York shoe designer Stuart Weitzman) and has gone through seizures, legal disputes and even secret service operations.

Some of these coins were not eliminated and in 2003 there were ten specimens around the world. Nine were tracked down and destroyed by the secret services, but the last coin survived and was owned by King Farouk of Egypt. It was auctioned off and sold for $7.6 million.

Brasher Doubloon

A very rare US doubloon of eight scudi worth $16, privately minted in 1787 and in the immediately following years.

The Brasher Doubloon is a solid gold coin weighing over 26 grams. It was created by a well-known goldsmith of the time who engraved his initials above it, we are talking about Ephraim Brasher. The request for this coin came to the State of New York from the goldsmith Ephraim Brasher, a neighbor of George Washington: it a pity that the upper levels of the government did not like the proposed design, the eagle and the Catskill mountains, and nobody wanted coins in copper. Brasher went his own way and continued to mint, both in bronze and in 22-karat gold.

This coin was sold in 2011 for $7.4 million to an investment company that wanted to remain secret.

Edward III

The Edward III coin was a coin in use from December 1343 to July 1344, it is a rare gold example.

The British gold florin of 1343, wanted by Edward III before the wide diffusion of the Noble, is one of the most expensive coins in the world: there are only three examples in the world and two are owned by the British Museum in London, founded by some students on the River Tyne in 1857

It has an almost absolute degree of gold purity and is also called Double Leopard because leopards are depicted on both the obverse and reverse, as happened with the lions on the gold coins of Theodosius I and on some imperial Roman coins.

It is estimated that there are only three copies in the world, and one of them sold for $6.80.

Gold Dinar

The Gold Dinar is a gold coin of medieval origin that was minted around 700 by an Arab caliph of the Umayyad dynasty. The coin weighs 4.25 grams and was made with gold extracted from the mine owned by the caliph. In 2011 this piece was sold by an anonymous European buyer for $6 million.

Liberty Head Nickel

The Liberty Head Nickel is a 5-cent coin issued around 1913, and produced in limited quantities, specifying that the United States Mint has never authorized its issue in any way, thus significantly increasing its value.

There are only 5 coins of this type, with the face of Liberty enclosed in stars on the obverse and the Roman V between ears of wheat and cotton branches on the reverse.

This nickel was minted without the approval of the Mint, which had changed the design of the piece: from that of the Liberty Head to the profile of a native and the Black Diamond bison.

It is a unique coin, it is estimated that there are only five copies in the world, two of which are placed in American museums. The other three are privately owned and one of these sold for over $4.5 million in 2018.

1804 silver dollar from the Queller's collection

The 1-dollar silver coin, known as "The King of American Coins", was not actually minted in 1804 but 30 years later: at the request of President Andrew Jackson, it was used as a gift for sultans and emirs during the travels of the diplomat Edmund Roberts between Thailand and Oman.

Its most massive distribution begins between 1834 and 1835. It was precisely in the decades following the first production of 1804 that collectors became aware of the existence of the so-called Class I coins and began to seek in every possible way to obtain them.

The 1804 silver dollar from the Queller's collection was minted in 1835 and weighs 26.98 grams, was entrusted to Heritage and sold in 2008 for $3.7 million.

50 lire of Vittorio Emanuele II of 1864

One of the rarest coins of the Kingdom of Italy, minted in just 103 specimens. This 50-lire gold coin has on the obverse the profile of the sovereign (with the date below and the name of the designer below the neck: Giuseppe Ferraris) and on the reverse, the Savoy coat of arms crowned and adorned with the collar of the Annunziata between two branches of 'laurel, with the value and the mintmarks below. In May 2017, on the Bolaffi "Coins, banknotes and medals" auction in Turin, it was sold for 225,700 euros starting from a base of 150,000.

The 2007 Big Maple Leaf

It is the huge Canadian 1-million-dollar coin: its weight is 100 kilograms in almost pure gold (99.99%), so much so that it ended up in the Guinness Book of Records for its incomparable degree of purity. Minted in a set of six by the Royal Canadian Mint, it features the profile of Queen Elizabeth II (by Canadian artist Susanna Blunt) on the obverse and the iconic maple leaf (by engraver Stan Witten) on the reverse. In June 2010 it was auctioned in Vienna for 3,145,000 euros, while in March 2017 it was subject to an incredible theft in Germany: a gang of thieves of Lebanese origin stole it from the Münzkabinett of the Bode Museum in Berlin, entering the museum with a ladder from a window. The joke is that the insurance paid just 20% of the value of the coin, claiming that the fault of the theft was attributable to the negligence of the staff. Only after a lawsuit, the insurance company was ordered to increase the compensation to 50%.

Umayyad gold dinar from 723

Minted in Damascus during the second of the four caliphates established after Muhammad's death, probably on the Hajj pilgrimage to Mecca, this coin set an all-time record in the Arab world: in 2020 it was auctioned by Morton & Eden in London for 5,120,000 euros. It is also the first gold dinar to make explicit reference to a place, today's Saudi Arabia, and to a mine owned by the caliph himself, dug on land acquired by direct descent from the Prophet.

CHAPTER 3: TOP COUNTERFEITED COINS IN THE WORLD

Counterfeit coins are all those coins that, even if they appear similar or apparently the same as those minted by the Bank, are slightly different.

The art of counterfeiting dates to the time of the use of the first coins. In the beginning, the aim was to deceive farmers or traders by using counterfeit coins which then easily entered circulation.

Now, and especially as regards the coin collecting market, counterfeiters are manufacturing classic coins, which are no longer in circulation, to deceive collectors by selling high-priced pieces that don't even exist anymore.

In practice, a counterfeit coin is any type of coin that is produced by a private individual without the country where the coin is minted being aware of this production or having ever authorized its production.

If your goal is to start collecting coins, then you need to start protecting yourself from counterfeiting. To avoid all this, there are 4 useful tips that you must always follow:

- Only purchase coins certified by a third-party-operated coin grading service.

- Find a qualified and experienced coin dealer in your area and purchase your collectible coins only from that dealer.

- Do not buy coins that are sold at prices too low compared to their market value, especially if you find these coins online or in flea markets.

- If you have aimed at a collector's coin, but for some reason, you believe that this is a fake, contact a more experienced person who will be able to remove any doubts.

That said, counterfeit coins fall into three main categories:

- Struck Counterfeits, in this case, the counterfeiters produce coins with the same procedure that the Mint uses to mint the coins which then go into circulation. The counterfeiter creates the die-cut coins by manually engraving them using an engraving lathe with the one-to-one transfer, to create counterfeit coins identical to the originals. As one of the most complicated and expensive methods of minting coins, this method is only used for minting high-value coins.

- Cast Counterfeits is a cheaper method to counterfeit coins than the previous one and consists in recreating the mold of the authentic coin and using it to melt the coin which will then be counterfeited. Counterfeiters prefer this method as the process does not destroy the host coin. When the molds are ready, the molten metal is a dip on top. In any case, however, expert counterfeiters may be, the result is always of poor quality.

- Altered and Doctored Coins, among the three methods, are certainly the cheapest and fastest for counterfeiters to make money at the expense of coin collectors. The counterfeiting method is quite simple, you take a regular coin and modify it just enough to make it look rare and expensive. For example, a skilled forger may add a mark or detail to the coin or remove a minor detail to make it appear more expensive than it actually is. Another very common example of this type of counterfeit is divided coins. In this case, the forger will take two common coins, split them in two and then weld the two halves together. In this way, whoever goes to buy the coin will have the illusion of having a rare and expensive coin in their hands.

Mostly common counterfeited USA coins

In this paragraph, you will be shown which are the most famous counterfeit coins in the USA.

1909-S VDB Lincoln Cent

This is definitely one of the most popular US collectible coins. For this reason, this coin has become the most counterfeited and altered collector's coin in the world. Very often in these coins, a small detail is added such as, for example, the S of the Mint or the initials V.D.B., to lead to the highest valuation ever for this coin.

1916-D Mercury Dime

The key date of the very popular Mercury Dime series of coins is 1916. The popularity of this coin has meant that many collectors also bought it for quite significant sums.
This coin is one of the most common and affordable around. For this reason, counterfeiters just add the mintmark D to make the common coin look like a rare coin.

1914 Indian $2.50

The 1914 Gold Quarter Eagle is the second-lowest mintage in the famous Indian Head series. In fact, only 240 thousand pieces were minted and for this reason, they are highly sought after by collectors, especially if they are still in mint condition. Due to the great attention paid to these coins in the collectors' market, unfortunately, there have been many counterfeits already circulating since the 1960s. Most counterfeits involve heavy blows of counterfeiting into the back of the neck of the figure depicted in the coin.

1914-D Lincoln Cent

While this cent is not as popular as the 1909-S VDB, this coin actually has strong popularity among coin collectors. For this reason, this cent is one of the primary targets in the reality of counterfeiting. The major types of counterfeiting concern the addition of the D as a mintmark. Or another way they use to counterfeit this coin is the alterations of the minting dates.

1882 Indian $3

The counterfeit of this 3-dollar coin best known in the world of collectors is the one called Omega Man. The name derives from the fact that counterfeiters add a tiny Omega symbol to the counterfeit coin, especially in the R of the word LIBERTY. Most of these counterfeits were created in the 1970s but are still circulating in collector coins today.

Mostly common counterfeited Worldwide coins

After talking about the most counterfeit coins in the history of the United States, let's see which are the most counterfeit coins in the world.

Korea KK501 (1892) 5 Yang

This coin was minted with an annual circulation and consists of only 20,000 pieces. Thanks to its rarity due to the limited mintage, this is one of the most sought-after coins for both Asian and international collectors. All this attention and demand has increased the value of this coin, but also attracted many counterfeiters who have really worked to reproduce this rare piece. The most common type of counterfeiting of this currency is transfer die.

Great Britain 1775 Halfpenny

This 1775 coin has the typical design of earlier Tower Mints, featuring King George wearing armor on the obverse of the coin and Britannia on the reverse holding a spear and an olive branch.
During the reign of King George III, half pennies were rarely minted, and the lack of change created serious problems and tensions within the country. The rarity of these coins has led to their heavy counterfeiting. In fact, it is estimated that in 1780 only 8% of the coins in circulation were authentic. The main type of counterfeit found in these coins is the transfer-die counterfeit.

Vietnam 1945 20 Xu

This celebrative coin is quite popular and sought after in the collecting world. It is the first coin celebrating communism in Vietnam, making it a rare and highly valued historical piece. The problem with this coin is that the originals have already been minted in a coarse and approximate way, making it easier to counterfeit. Counterfeiting is easily recognizable, as counterfeit parts are better than the originals. The most common method of counterfeiting is transfer-die; however, some counterfeit pieces have scratches that streak, and drawings present in the coins.

Great Britain 1847 Gothic Crown

The coin is a gothic-styled crown with a deep cameo which makes it fascinating and highly sought after by collectors worldwide. The coin is in silver from 1847 and portrays Queen Victoria.

On the reverse of the coin are crowned cruciform shields and, in the corners, the national floral emblems.

The coin is very popular and is valued in thousands of dollars in most cases. For this reason, it has become one of the most popular coins among counterfeiters. However, counterfeits are easily recognizable as counterfeit coins lack the details that are found in real coins. A striking example of counterfeiting can be seen in the part with the design of the three lions on the reverse of the coin. The authentic pieces in this part of the coin have a characteristic swelling in the lower part of the shield where the three lions are impressed, while in the counterfeit coins, this swelling is completely missing.

Italy 1936R XIV 20 Lire

This ancient Italian coin was minted to celebrate King Vittorio Emanuele III of Italy and was issued by the Mint of Rome in 1936 to celebrate the constitution of the Empire together with the other pieces in the series.

In total, only 10,000 pieces were minted, and the rarity of this coin makes it particularly attractive to collectors from all over the world. Furthermore, it is highly appreciated for its classic design and aesthetic appearance. The high demand and rarity of the coin drove up prices and increased the production of counterfeit pieces.

Most counterfeits involve printing the coins with older transfer dies than the original. Although the coins appear to be of high quality, they have raised points emerging from the reeds.

CHAPTER 4: MOST VALUABLE ERROR COINS

As we said in the 4th book, minting errors are one of the most appreciated aspects for coin collectors. These unconventional-looking coins can turn out to be real treasures.

In this chapter, we will go to see which are the most valued coins with minting errors both belonging to the US and international markets.

Most US Valuable Error Coins

What you will find listed below are the most valued flawed coins in the US market.

1975 No S Proof Roosevelt Dime

The US Mint included in the 1975 proof coins these Dimes which had a particular error, they were missing the mintmark S, which stood for the city of San Francisco. To be precise, these truly rare coins are only produced for the annual mint-proof sets. The flawed coin is rare and valuable as only two examples exist in the world and prices go up to $450,000.

2000-P Sacagawea Dollar + Washington Quarter Mule

Mules are one of the strangest and most hilarious minting errors to be found on a coin. The two-dollar Sacagawea Mule is certainly the most loved and known of all the coins that have this type of error.

The coin was struck on a planchet from the 2000 gold dollar coins, but the reverse of the coin was combined with the obverse of a Washington quarter. The completely accidental error is very beautiful on an aesthetic level both for the gold color and for the similar dimensions of the two-coin denominations.

There are a total of 19 examples in circulation and they are practically all new and immaculate pieces. For this reason, the average price of these coins is around 50,000 dollars.

1944 Steel Lincoln Cent

All coin collectors know that during the Second World War the USA, to deal with the war industry, had to negatively impact the production of coins, especially copper and nickel coins. Nickels from 5 cents were converted using an alloy containing 35% silver in the years 1942 to 1945, while pennies were converted, starting in 1943, to a zinc-coated steel alloy.

Over 1 billion of these steel alloy cents were produced in 1943, however, due to the high production numbers it happens that a small number of coins, about 15, were struck incorrectly on a bronze planchet. These rare bronze cents, in addition to being rare, are highly sought after by collectors also for their aesthetic appearance and, considering these two elements together, they have meant that the price of these coins with minting error exceeded the threshold of 100 thousand dollars.

1974-D Aluminum Lincoln Cent

The existence of this error-minting penny remained virtually unknown to collectors around the world until 2001.

Throughout the mid-1900s, the US Mint used all sorts of materials to mint coins. Finally, in 1982, the Treasury Department selected copper-plated zinc as the minting material for this Lincoln effigy penny. Before choosing this alloy for the minting of the coin, Congress had opted for pieces in aluminum, but the coin was immediately rejected. However, about 12 pieces escaped government control in 1974. To date, however, only 2 pieces exist in circulation. One of the two copies has become the property of the government, while the second is currently worth a 5-figure figure.

1982 No P Roosevelt Dime

Some coins belonging to the 1982 minting of the Philadelphia Mint belonging to the Roosevelt series were created with a circulation strike. The Mint added the letter P to the 10-centime coin in 1980. Coins prior to this date did not bear any mintmark. Some coins, in 1982, were created by mistake without the letter P on the obverse. Several thousand of these coins circulated before realizing the mistake. Even if it seems a huge figure, it must however be remembered that the total minting of the coins of that year could not exceed 520,000 units and for this reason, these thousands of coins are considered a rarity.

In fact, there are collectors willing to pay up to $175 for a 10-cent coin.

Most valuable worldwide errors coins

After seeing the most valued coins with mint errors in the United States, below you will find a list of the most valued coins with mint errors in the world:

Australia 1974 20 Cent Split Planchet Error Mated Pair VF

This Australian 20-cent coin was minted in Australia in 1974. The coin is split into two halves and both halves were fused together during minting. In minting errors, it is easy to find a split planchet but seeing a pair of coins paired as in this case is quite unusual. Thanks to this minting error, the coin is valued at up to 450 Australian dollars.

Canada 1969 dollar transitional off-metal struck on silver 50c planchet pl65

This Canadian coin is a transitional and off-metal coin, as it was minted on a silver half-dollar planchet. Canada then stopped minting silver half dollars after 1967. However, some quite rare silver dollars were minted in 1969. This coin is quite rare and prized not only because it was created on a metal that was not more used for 2 years but also because it was therefore minted on the wrong plate, i.e., the half-dollar one instead of the one-dollar one. The valuation of this coin is around 5000 dollars.

Italian 2002 1cent coin

In 2002, the Italian State Mint accidentally minted about a thousand 1-cent coins on a planchet of 2 cents, using, in practice, the wrong mold to mint the coin. In these wrong 1-cent coins there is the Mole Antonelliana of Turin on the reverse of the coin with Castel del Monte in Puglia on the front which was usually minted on the reverse of the coins. Although the Italian State has tried in every way to withdraw these coins, some have remained in circulation, eventually ending up at auction houses. Although the initial value of these coins is 2500 euros there have been examples that have been auctioned for 6000 euros.

CHAPTER 5: BULLIONS COINS TO CONSIDER FOR A COIN COLLECTING BUSINESS

As we learned from the 4th book of this series, bullion coins are economic solutions used to invest and make profits.

Bullion coins can differ from other types of gold investments by various factors. You must know that bullion coins that have a gold purity higher than 900 thousandths and that have been minted after 1800 must be sold at a price that is not higher than 80% of the value on the free market of the gold found in them. For example, the pound, the Italian, Austrian or Swiss Marenghi, are the most purchased coins for these reasons. When referring to investment gold, the numismatic value must always be taken into consideration. In practice, the gold coin will be taken into consideration for its percentage of gold.

To understand what the value of gold coins is and understand if they are authentic pieces, you must first check the current price of gold based on the gram, then you can check the various tables on the net with all the main gold coins.

What are the best investment gold coins?

There are many gold investment coins known in the world. The best bullion coins are the following:

- 1 Austrian Ducat, with a total weight of 3.49 grams
- American Eagle
- 10 dollars Liberty gold coin weighing 16.718 grams
- 20 Liberty Gold dollars of 33.436 grams
- 4 Austrian ducats of 13.96 grams
- 10 Mexican pesos for 8.33 grams
- 100 Austrian crowns of 33.8753 grams
- Krugerrand of 33.933 grams
- Marenghi weighing 6.451 grams
- 7.988-gram pound
- Kangaroo from 1/20 of an ounce to 1kg
- Maple leaf.

Gold pounds are the most common coin and can also be purchased at banks or specialty shops. Gold Sovereigns can also be sold using channels other than banking.

A gold pound is worth 3% to 15% more than the gold price. If you buy an American Eagle, you can sell it from a base price of $50 all the way up to $1,600.

Let's see in detail some of these coins that you can collect for future investment.

Austrian Ducat

The Golden Austrian Ducat is a coin minted by the Austrian mint, namely the Münze Osterreich. It is also called "education" as opposed to the "education", i.e., the 4 Ducati coin, also produced by the mint of Austria.

It is a very light coin, its weight is in fact only 3.490 grams, of which 3.442 are gold, with a purity of 98.61%. The diameter is 20mm.

The obverse of the coin depicts Emperor Franz Joseph with his head surrounded by laurel. The inscription "FRANC IOS I D G AUSTRIAE IMPERATOR" is impressed around the profile portrait of the emperor.

The reverse of the Golden Duchy of Austria shows the Austrian shield superimposed on the crowned double-headed eagle with the inscription HUNGAR BOHEM GAL LOD ILL REX 1915 around it, to celebrate the other territories over which the emperor reigned.

The coin was minted by the Austrian mint from 1831 to 1915, but every specimen still in circulation bears the latter date. In fact, each re-mint was dated 1915 even if that was not the actual year of the re-mint.

The Golden Duchy of Austria is a specimen highly sought after by collectors above all because it belongs to a past historical period, which saw Austria-Hungary as one of the predominant states in Europe.

20 Dollar Liberty Head gold coin

The 20 US dollar gold coin was minted from 1850 to 1907 by the United States Mint. The coin is also called the Liberty Head because Liberty is represented on the obverse in the form of a woman, as is the case on the 5- and 10-dollar coins.

In the first part of American republican history, only 2.50-, 5- and 10-dollar coins were minted, and no thought was given to producing any multiples due to lack of gold availability.

With the conquest of the West and the discovery of large gold deposits in California, the US Congress approved the minting of the 20 US dollar coin in 1849. They were also called "Double Eagles" because their face value was double that of the "Eagle", i.e., the 10-dollar coins.

The total weight of the US $20 is 33.44 grams, of which 30.09 grams is gold, therefore providing the coin with 90% purity. The remaining 10% is made up of copper, which is necessary to make the coin resistant to wear. The diameter of the gold coin is 34 millimeters.

On the obverse, we find 13 stars around the figure of Liberty, representing the 13 colonies that later became independent from Great Britain. The date of minting is stamped under the neck of the woman's profile.

On the reverse is an eagle with spread wings clawing arrows and an olive branch. A square-shaped shield is drawn on the chest of the eagle.

The words "UNITED STATES OF AMERICA" are engraved on the upper part of the reverse, while the face value of the coin is engraved in the letters "TWENTY DOLLARS", i.e., 20 dollars, on the lower part.

10 Mexican Gold Pesos

The 10 gold Mexican pesos are a coin minted from 1921 to 1947 by the Casa de Moneda de México, i.e., the Mint of Mexico. 1921 is the year of the beginning of the production of Mexican pesos and has a particularly symbolic value, 1921 corresponds in fact to the centenary of Mexico's independence from Spain.

One of the protagonists of Mexican independence was Don Miguel Hidalgo, whose portrait is present on the obverse of the 2.5 gold Mexican pesos. Also called Padre Hidalgo or Father of the Homeland, Don Miguel Hidalgo is considered the initiator of the war that led Mexico to become independent from Spain.

The Mexican gold 10 peso, therefore, has a strong patriotic appeal, as do all other denominations of the Mexican gold peso. Before the arrival of the Krugerrand on international markets, the Mexican peso was a very popular currency and interest was global. Although the coinage was terminated in 1947, the 10 Mexican pesos were used by citizens as circulating currency until the 1970s.

Subsequently, this became almost impossible due to the rise in the value of gold, which led the holders to no longer use these coins as current currency, but as an investment product.

Now let's move on to the characteristics of the gold coin. It weighs 8.33 grams, of which 7.50 grams of gold, its fineness in thousandths is 900/1,000, this means that the coin is made up of 90% gold and therefore falls within the investment. The diameter is 22.48 mm, while the face value is precisely 10 Mexican pesos.

On the obverse we find the portrait of Father Hidalgo, on his left in a circle we have the inscription "DIEZ PESOS", which continues on the right side with the addition of the date of minting.

On the reverse is drawn the eagle, which is the Mexican national symbol and is present in the flag of Mexico. The eagle has a snake in its beak, which wants to reproduce the way in which the Mexican people achieved independence, that is by fighting proudly.

10 dollars Liberty gold coin

The 10 American gold Liberty dollar coin was minted from 1838 to 1907 by the United States Mint. The coin is also called Eagle, due to the presence of the bird on the back of the gold coin.

This coin also takes the name of Liberty Head because on the obverse there is the personification of liberty in the form of a woman seen in profile, the design was created by James B. Longacre, chief engraver of the US Mint at the time.

The total weight of the Liberty 10 US Gold Dollars is 16.71 grams, of which 15.04 grams is gold, therefore giving the coin 21.6 carats since it is 90% gold purity. The remaining 10% is made up of copper, which is necessary to make the coin resistant to wear. The diameter of the gold coin is 27 millimeters.

On the obverse, we find 13 stars around the figure of Liberty, which are none other than the 13 colonies which later became independent from Great Britain. The 13 stars are also featured on the US flag. The date of minting is stamped under the neck of the woman's profile.

On the reverse is an eagle with spread wings clawing arrows and an olive branch. On the chest of the eagle, we find instead a square-shaped shield.

The words "UNITED STATES OF AMERICA" are engraved on the upper part of the reverse of the 10 American gold Liberty dollars, while the face value of the coin is engraved in the letters "TEN DOLLARS", i.e., 10 dollars, on the lower part.

CONCLUSION

With these five guides, we have to learn everything about coins, before starting to collect them.

We have seen their anatomy, material, value and what is necessary to understand if a coin is counterfeit or true.

We learned about collecting coins and how to do it from zero. what are the coins that are with minting errors?

All this is to make you understand that starting to collect coins is definitely a fun, exciting and exciting practice.

But that can become a real business if you correctly recognize the value that your collection can assume and the right time to sell.

Starting with current or modern coins you will be able to understand what you are most passionate about. Then progressively go to collect older and older coins. You could even go as far as ancient coins like Roman coins or Greek coins. In this way, you will increase the historical and investment value of your coin collection more and more.

Made in United States
Troutdale, OR
07/14/2023